Running a successful wedding DJ business

"It's not what you do, it's how you do it!"
– *Mark Ferrell*

Wedding Marketing for DJs

John Beck   Derek Pengelly

FOREWORD BY
MARK FERRELL

What's your potential? What's your real potential? Not some far off imaginary wish or impossible dream. What are you really capable of? Are you capable of great things – big things? Do you have a vision for yourself and those you serve? Is it achievable? How do you know if it is or if it isn't?

You can't base your success or abilities upon what others do, can you? If that were true, no new records would ever be set. No new products would be invented. Roger Bannister would not have broken the four-minute mile because no one had ever done that before. It was believed that it was humanly impossible and that perhaps severe injury would result from trying. Steve Jobs would have never created Apple computers, the Macintosh, the iPod, iTunes, the iPhone, and the iPad. No one had ever done anything like it before. If they had waited to see if someone else could do it, they would have never even tried.

So what can you do?

For many years, the definition of "Mobile DJ" has been limited and stifled by those who see the role in only one dimension. This perception was passed on to the public, so the public expected a very limited role and value for mobile DJs. And thus, the image and price expectation were set… and set low, indeed.

In 1989, my wife and I shattered the traditional definition of "Mobile DJ" when we started our Mobile DJ business, specialising in weddings and charged five times the "going rate." At a time when very few mobile DJs were using a microphone, we acted as a true Master of Ceremonies, invented concepts like The Love Story, Expanded Personalised Grand Entrances, Custom slide shows with voice recordings, and sound drops. We used staging, entertainment pacing, and coordination to achieve spectacular results – all of this, in addition to the more traditional role as music provider.

Gladly, now these concepts are becoming accepted more as the role of "Mobile DJ" and don't seem so far-fetched as they once were, thanks in part to mentorship, associations, conventions, workshops, seminars, and books such as this one.

John and Derek have compiled information from a variety of sources in one, complete, holistic compendium that will spark your imagination and creativity. It will help further define "Mobile DJ" and the "industry." But most importantly, it will start you on a path to achieving your potential and expanding your capabilities.

You see, this is just a beginning; a cursory view of what's possible in a new paradigm that you create. Because, after all, it's YOUR potential, which cannot be created by anyone else, any more than you can achieve someone else's potential.

So I ask again – no – I implore, what can YOU do?

I hope that this book will inspire you to do amazing things; to shine spectacularly; and to continue to redefine the role of "Mobile DJ" and create lasting, meaningful memories for those you serve.

As Katy Perry sang, "Baby, you're a firework. Come on, show 'em what you're worth! Make 'em go oh, oh, oh!"

There you are. Sitting. Waiting. Stationary. Silent in your mortar. The potential to reach great heights and explode into awe-striking beauty and excitement. You've been shaped, packed, arranged - fuse added.

You. Are. Ready. YOU Are.

Your Potential is dormant, as long as you wait doing nothing. Your Worth isn't yet realised while inside the tube. The fuse must be lit. You must be propelled. Come on, dear DJs! Let's show 'em what you're Worth!!

Mark Ferrell
The MarBecca Method
www.markferrell.com
©2014 MarBecca Entertainment

About Mark Ferrell

Mark Ferrell is the leading and most respected speaker, trainer, and advocate for the mobile DJ industry worldwide, having presented keynotes, seminars, and workshops in more than 50 cities in the U.S., in the United Kingdom, Australia, and in Canada, and has keynoted several national and international industry conventions.

Recognized as the mentor and trainer to the top earning performers in the industry (the trainer's trainer), Mark has received acclaim by peers in the profession and honours including induction into the American DJ Association's Hall of Fame, Mobile Beat Magazine's Lifetime Achievement Award, the ADJA President's Award, the ADJA Outstanding Achievement Award, and Mobile Beat's All Star's Award.

It's amazing to think how many current authors, coaches, seminar givers, workshop providers, etc. have all learnt under the MarBecca umbrella.

I highly recommend every DJ listen to the Getting What You're Worth seminar. You can download it from www.markferrell.com

CONTENTS

ACKNOWLEDGMENTS

A heartfelt thank you is extended to the many talented DJs I have met over the years. I am extremely grateful for all that they have shared with me and ultimately with you. All of the people listed on page 151 have contributed to this book in one way or another. Ideas shared in their books, websites or video presentations have shaped the way I operate as a mobile DJ. It is difficult to be specific as to which ideas came from whom. I would thank them all for their work and give credit where it is due.

I had no idea just how much one person has influenced me in the way I perform as a DJ and master of ceremonies both directly and indirectly in the last 4 years, until I put this book together. I just had to single him out - it's Mark Ferrell.

The term, "It's not what you do, it's how you do it," has been the MarBecca Method slogan for the past 8 years. It's a theme throughout the book and I would like to acknowledge that it is a term devised by Mark and extend my thanks for allowing me to use it.

.

ABOUT THE AUTHORS

John Beck

"What do you want to do for a career, Johnny?" asked the careers counsellor. I thought about it for a few days, and at 15 years of age I wanted the easiest job I could think of: a radio DJ!

In 1983 I did work experience at a Melbourne radio station, 92.3 EON FM (now MMM), and also established and ran the college radio station, before studying at Clark Sinclair's Radio School. That landed me my first job in radio as the office assistant at 3KZ (now GOLD FM). I was there for 17 months doing everything from photocopying to producing commercials and editing pre-recorded shows.

To cut a long story short, my on-air career never made it to fruition and with two friends I started a mobile DJ business. We were too young and inexperienced at that time to make a living from DJing and had to get a job. For me it was in retail and while at the time I didn't like it much, I did learn a lot about customer service and how customers think when they shop, which helps me now running my business as a wedding DJ and Master of Ceremonies.

Since then I have worked for several larger DJ companies and seen how they operate. I've DJed all sorts of private functions including nightclubs in Melbourne, Sydney, Las Vegas and San Francisco. But I got the most satisfaction from seeing how much fun the brides and grooms were having and how much they appreciated my help and service. I have now found my passion in weddings and, since 2011, I no longer do any other functions.

I believe a wedding is the most challenging and rewarding event a mobile DJ can do. Challenging as two people have trusted you with their once-in-a-lifetime event, they have asked you to stand up in front of their closest friends and family and take responsibility for their reception. So you had better get it right. Rewarding when the couple send you a thank you and talk about the impact you personally had in making their day so special and memorable, in more ways than just playing music.

I found my passion for weddings after my first trip to America to attend the Mobile Beat DJ conference in Las Vegas in 2009. There I met some very talented, passionate and inspiring people, who showed me how serious they were about their craft.

I returned again in 2011 to attend more seminars where I discovered I could do intense training workshops to improve my skills in all aspects of entertainment and to start working on becoming a true Master of Ceremonies entertainer and DJ.

I'm sure you will find something in this book to help you become a better DJ and in the end the clients will benefit, because that's what it's all about.

There is always something you can improve upon.

Derek Pengelly

Otherwise known as David Summers, Derek is 56 and married to Carol. They have recently left the United Kingdom to seek a more relaxed and balanced lifestyle abroad. Derek has been a mobile DJ since his late teens when DJs had little choice but to build their own equipment and pursue a hobby which occasionally paid them a bob or two.

In the early years a limited range of equipment was available. There were only a small number of companies building DJ consoles. FAL, Carlsboro, Simms-watt and Citronic spring to mind, together with some specialist suppliers like Roger Squires in London and Sound Advice Installations (SAI) of Wigan.

Over the years Derek has provided music for just about every conceivable occasion. Youth clubs, social clubs, pubs, church and village halls, hotels of all grades and sizes, Masonic Lodges, private clubs; you name them and Derek has played them. Likewise he has covered christenings, birthday parties, engagements, marriages, funerals, presentation award nights, theme nights, tribute nights; again, the list is endless. However, the one type of event Derek came to specialise in was weddings.

This was just as well because over the years on many occasions he was sent by an agent to provide entertainment for a party with very little information provided other than the location and the name of the client. Imagine his surprise when greeted by a bride asking if he had their 'first dance' record. This could have been a huge problem; back in the good old days (no MP3s or downloads available) there was less music to choose from; however, Derek carried an extensive collection of 'first dance' songs which usually saved the day. He quickly learnt that he needed to be flexible and prepared for any eventuality. He thought, "There must be a better way than this", which prompted him to strive for better client communications and pre-event consultations which would lead to more controlled, planned and structured parties without unexpected stress for all concerned.

Like the majority of mobile DJs Derek had a day job. His career in electrical retail started at a time when cassette tapes had only just been developed. Derek worked on the high street as a salesman and store manager for Currys Ltd. During this time he saw the launch of the first calculators, electronic watches, home computers, games consoles, video recorders, music centres, portable televisions and mobile phones. His responsibilities included training staff and achieving sales and profit growth. He later moved on to work with other leading retailers before joining General Motors where he had a spell in production before becoming a commercial vehicle sales advisor covering the north west of England. This experience was to prove very useful when it came to running his entertainment company.

Weddings are his passion. He has travelled thousands of miles seeking information, education and training – yes, training – in order to be able to produce fantastic, fun and memorable wedding DJ entertainment. This enabled him to offer premium wedding services for discerning couples at fees often two, three or four times higher than the local average.

Back in 1990 Carol joined him in the business and they founded David Summers & Co Entertainment Ltd. The business was a success providing quality DJ entertainment to local hotels in the north west of England. Derek was constantly looking for help with marketing and performance skills but found very little in the UK. In 2002 Carol and Derek took a leap of faith and travelled to Las Vegas to attend a Mobile DJ convention. Mobile Beat changed their perception of the DJ industry and was the beginning of an adventure which is still paying dividends today.

At this convention Derek's eyes were opened. Here he found dozens of mobile DJs who were prepared to share their ideas and better still industry leading mentors who were able to teach and train those willing to learn. People such as Mark Ferrell, Peter Merry, DJ Doctor Drax, Randy Bartlett, Jim Cerone and many more, all willing to share their expertise. However, it became obvious from the start that this sharing came at a price. In return for receiving all of this knowledge Derek had one obligation which was to pass it on down the line.

Upon his return to the UK, Derek set about finding likeminded DJs around the country and eventually found what was then the Thames Valley Disc

Jockey Association. However, in order to reach more people it became apparent that the association needed to become larger and attract more members. In 2004 the organisation changed its name and the National Association of Disc Jockeys was born. In 2005 Derek became its chairman and the process began of spreading the word by offering education and training to DJs around the country. More recently Derek has written articles for Pro Mobile Magazine and presented independent seminars and workshops around the country. Derek could also be seen attending and supporting DJ Show North, NADJ trade shows and the BPM show.

He is passionate about weddings. Weddings are special. They are unique. It is his belief that many brides are 'sold short' when it comes to entertainment. Many organisations, especially multi-site international hotel chains, have reduced weddings to little more than an expensive meal. Brides need to be empowered. Weddings should be fun and memorable. The entertainment should start from the moment the bride arrives at the venue. His company, David Summers Entertainment, established itself as an innovative producer of memorable wedding receptions.

Today Derek is helping DJs in the United Kingdom to follow in his footsteps. He has created and produced a series of workshops for mobile DJs who wish to specialise as wedding DJs. These workshops cover all aspects of the wedding DJ business. They offer help with marketing, administration, sales, planning, performance and business development.

Way back in 2002 he thought he knew it all. How wrong he was. The more he learnt the more he realised he didn't know. The process of education and perfecting your skills is ongoing and never-ending. Professional sportsmen and women need a coach. Actors frequently take master-classes from their peers. Why is it that most DJs are self-taught and seldom seek training? Is it because there is none available or do they believe they don't need help?

The best piece of advice given to Derek came from Mark Ferrell.

"If you want to know how much you are worth as a wedding DJ, simply fail to turn up at your next wedding reception. You won't be sued for the amount of your fee; you'll be sued for the cost of ruining the entire party."

Thank you for buying this book.
Hopefully you will find inspiration and value within its pages

1] WHY WEDDINGS?

It's a good question. Why single out weddings when there are so many other parties or events which a mobile DJ can perform at? Personally, I believe that a wedding is the most challenging and rewarding type of event for a mobile DJ. Let's just take a look as to why that is.

A typical wedding in Australia usually, but not always, requires a mobile DJ to turn up and play music at the reception. Your instructions are normally to turn up and set up while the venue staff are putting the final touches to the room and getting ready for the arrival of guests. You will then be expected to play background music during dinner for anything from two to three hours.

Traditionally the bride and groom will have the first dance and open the dancing for friends and family; you may eventually get your full dance floor and a party atmosphere sometime after 9.00 p.m.

Think about this! What about the guests who are not dancers and never will be, or can't dance due to age, illness or injury? How are they going to have fun and enjoy the reception? They are there because they have been invited, period. They will like a drink or two and a chat if volume levels permit and they may well have their own agenda which includes leaving early. As for the other guests, what kind of music do they like? There will be so many age groups and different types of music requested that trying to include everyone and ensure a great entertainment experience is a monumental challenge. This can be quite daunting and explains why so many mobile DJs choose not to specialise in this type of party or, worse still, totally ignore all of these factors and treat a wedding reception just like any other party.

Experience suggests that everyone loves a wedding: people will travel from the other side of the world to attend, people take days off work; if you don't realise already, a wedding is a BIG deal!! Therefore a great wedding DJ needs to understand the challenge he or she is undertaking.

This book will guide you through the process of understanding what makes a great wedding reception and how you can make it fun, unique and memorable. Your knowledge, expertise and professionalism will ensure that all the guests are included, entertained and thrilled by what you do.

A wedding DJ needs to be versatile. They also need to leave their ego at the door. A wedding reception is where the focus falls on the bride and groom.

The spotlight should be on them and their guests. Everything you do or say as a DJ should reflect their personality, mood and vision. I'm not suggesting the DJ not be interactive or vocal, quite the contrary; rather, I'm suggesting that he or she needs to tone down their performance and bring it into line with the event. The better wedding DJs actually change their levels of energy throughout the day or evening to mirror the reaction of the guests. I like to think of a wedding DJ slowly bringing a party to the boil. Gently simmering to begin with and knowing exactly when to turn up the heat!

"It's not what you do, it's how you do it"

The secret to successfully marketing your DJ services to brides and grooms is quite simple. "It's not what you do, it's how you do it" that makes a difference and gets results. A wedding is a one-off event, never to be repeated (hopefully) and therefore it is important to get it right. Organising a wedding can be very stressful and often results in a bride not being able to enjoy her big day. This is something we can help relieve or eliminate. Peace of mind and confidence instilled by a pro DJ can have an enormous effect on the guests and goes a long way to creating a relaxed and fun party. Why would a bride want to risk the success of her wedding reception to an amateur who did not understand the importance of working with her and not simply for her?

What are the advantages for you as a specialist wedding DJ?

Firstly, your added responsibility carries a premium valuation which will enable you to earn above-average fees for your services. You will be required to spend a great deal of time researching your clients' wants and needs. This pays dividends on the day of the reception and makes your music selection and interaction with the guests appear spontaneous and inspired.

Secondly, I would suggest that a specialist wedding DJ will produce, direct and oversee a different event on each occasion. This means never getting tired or stale and enjoying each party as though it was your first event.

Thirdly, when done correctly, you, the DJ, will find that bookings will become easier to find. Many other service providers such as photographers and videographers will be recommending you to their clients. Hotel duty managers and wedding coordinators will be keen to refer you. You will be able to reduce your dependence on advertising and will gather more and more business from word-of-mouth recommendation.

Finally, the rewards

Rewarding to me knowing I went to work that day and put that smile on the bride and groom's face, and made the guests laugh one minute and have them in tears of joy the next. I love it when the couple send me a thank you and talk about the impact I personally had in making their day so special and memorable, in more ways than just playing music. Here's just a few and as you will see they don't talk about how good the lights looked or the music and the way it was mixed.

"John Beck is a legend! I mean it with all my heart when I say he is the reason my wedding was the best, most elegant, entertaining party I have ever been to."

Melissa G.

"Our wedding was very unique and had things that our guests had never seen at a wedding before. Every moment was beautiful and we have John to thank for it."

Larissa and Ben C.

"I loved the moment John introduced our wedding dance – it was genuine and felt as though a friend was inviting us onto the dance floor."

Karli M.

There is practically no limit as to how much you can earn as a wedding DJ. Some clients want nothing less than the best money can buy. You could be that DJ. Take it from me, there are many DJs in Australia (2014) who regularly earn upwards of $3000 per wedding. Guess what? Very little of what they do has to do with playing music, but more about that later.

Your success as a wedding DJ will stretch you as a performer. A wedding DJ will be expected to make announcements; how good are your vocal skills? How you introduce the bride and groom will demonstrate their confidence in you and your command of the audience. How you stage-manage important ceremonies like the cutting of the cake and the first dance will determine whether or not everyone is included in the celebrations. There is nothing worse than important members of the bridal party being conspicuously absent from key formalities.

I guess it's easier to understand the key to providing great wedding entertainment when you compare it to the other alternative. Who wants an average or mediocre wedding reception? My friend Dave Windsor has a great line on his website which reads like this:

"A wedding reception without great entertainment is nothing more than a very expensive meal."

How many wedding receptions have you been invited to as a guest where you missed the bride and groom's first dance because the DJ didn't make the announcement, or if he did, no one heard it? How many times has the music been so loud no one could hear conversation so the guests moved out to the bar area, or worse, outside?! How many times has the DJ refused to play requests and played to an empty dance floor or maybe has played requests but only the ones he or she likes?

This book will enable you to understand that a wedding reception is not about you, it's about your client. Everything you say and do is through their eyes, in their style and has significance to them. Yes, you will use your personality and experience to turn their vision into reality but at the end of the day it is for the bride and groom to shine. You will be remembered as the one who made it all happen and the one who delivered more than their expectations. Yours will be the name on their lips when they are asked to recommend a great wedding DJ.

Just a mobile DJ?   Let's take a look at the many skills a mobile DJ has:
Music library
Music selection
Ability to read a dance floor / audience
Sound technician
Lighting technician
Event planner
Event coordinator
Entertainer
Font of all knowledge – you know where the cloakroom / toilets / light switches are, etc.
Microphone use – speeches, announcements, MC, etc.

When you think about it a mobile DJ has many talents which will enhance a wedding celebration. In many circumstances the DJ can, and does, do a better job of making announcements than a family member or venue employee. A DJ can use his music knowledge to add dynamics to an introduction or to add emotion to an announcement.

I believe that there is a whole new opportunity waiting for competent mobile DJs to get more involved with the other parts of a wedding day celebration which previously have been the domain of other service providers. Later we will look at these opportunities and explain just how you can use your skill and talent to create spectacular and memorable entertainment. It's not rocket science; it's simply a matter of taking responsibility and delivering great value.

Making a difference

Let's take a look at weddings in Australia today and look for opportunities where we as DJs can make a difference.

I believe that most of the wedding industry today has become a victim of faceless chain hotels who treat weddings as nothing more than an expensive meal. To them it is an opportunity to sell food and drink. What's more, they have dissected what was once an inclusive family occasion and compartmentalised the proceedings for their convenience at the expense of entertainment and enjoyment. Harsh words, I know, but hear me out.

Why is it that some venues have an objection to speeches before the meal?

I'll tell you. It's because they can't control the time those speeches will take and therefore the chef can't guarantee when the food will be served and the duty manager doesn't want to have the serving staff waiting around. It's much better for them to herd everyone in, sit them down and serve the food. Apart from the fact that this is the tail wagging the dog, why can't the bridal party have speeches before the meal if they choose to? Speeches first can be a great way to start the proceedings. Everyone gets to know the bride and groom's story and how it is we have arrived at this day. Conversation will flow afterwards and the whole room will be engrossed in the celebrations. I mean, just look at what happens traditionally. Everyone is sat down. The food is served to the sound of polite conversation and the clinking of cutlery. An hour and a half later the duty manager introduces the father of the bride and the speeches begin. Then just when everyone is getting into the festivities they announce the cutting of the cake, which is little more than a photo opportunity. (We'll come back to this later.) Then everyone is told to leave the room post-haste as the staff need to "turn the room around for the reception the next day". What's that all about?

Think about this. Who has more experience of talking to audiences – duty managers or you, the pro DJ? I would strongly argue that you can do a better job.

More importantly, your skill and talent coupled with MUSIC can make the whole experience a much more emotional, enjoyable and dynamic part of the celebrations. So why don't we get this opportunity?

Because no one knows that we can do it! The majority of brides and venue management still perceive mobile disc jockeys as 'music'. Don't get me wrong; MUSIC is important. A full dance floor is the goal for all of us to aspire to. However, a full dance floor is not necessarily the measuring stick by which to judge a wedding reception, especially if the dance floor measures no more than three square metres with 200 guests in the room.

First dances have also fallen victim to the production-line process adopted by many venues. The timing of a first dance is critical to us as DJs and to the way the whole evening's atmosphere is built and developed. Some venues still insist on first dances just before the main course. This creates all kinds of issues, not least the fact that no sooner is the first dance over than the lights are on and food is served. This can mean the party doesn't get a chance to get started until after ten o'clock.

The alternative at other venues is to hold the first dance back until after the dessert. This way there is no interruption once the dancing begins; however, this can still often mean waiting until after ten o'clock before the party springs into life. Some of the guests will have been waiting over three hours for this to happen. Why?

Surely the professional entertainer is best placed to advise when a first dance should take place and be able to produce and direct a stage-managed introduction which will be a highlight of the evening without having to apply a break for food just because it suits the caterers.

A mobile DJ who understands weddings and is prepared to work with a bride and groom to create a memorable wedding reception can and will be highly successful and respected for the professional that he or she is.

There are many opportunities where your skill and talent will contribute to outstanding wedding entertainment. More than just music, you have the power.

Together we will explore the possibilities and seek to show you how best to provide a unique service and create a wedding reception remembered for eternity (for all the right reasons).

It all comes down to education and communication. It's no use being the best wedding DJ on the block if nobody knows who you are or what you do.

Great wedding receptions don't just happen.

They are prepared like a gourmet meal. Only the best quality ingredients should be included in the mix. The recipe will be unique. You as the master chef will produce a veritable feast for all to enjoy. Everyone should be left contented, satisfied and delighted by the experience which you, the DJ, created.

In the following chapters I will help you understand your true worth and explain to you how I communicate value to potential clients.

2] UNDERSTANDING THE MARKET PLACE AND TARGET MARKETING

A market is a place where goods (products) or services are offered for sale. Understanding the market into which you want to sell your product or service is vital when it comes to pricing and how you position or present (package) your product or service. Here are a couple of non-DJ-related examples.

The traditional pie can be purchased in many places (markets). I can get into my car and drive to a supermarket and find numerous brands of pies at different prices. There will also be the supermarket's own-brand pie on sale for about $1. Or I could pop round to the corner shop and find only one brand of pie on sale for about $3. If I was travelling along a highway and fancied a pie and pulled into a service station I would find a lonely pie at a price over $4.

Here is another example. A glass of beer in a social club is currently about $3.50-$4.00. Yet in a chain brewery-run pub in a town centre the same glass will cost me nearer to $6. If I walk into a four- or five-star hotel you can bet that the same glass will cost upward of $7.

At the end of the day it's only a pie or a beer. What dictates the price is the market where they are sold. Strangely enough, I and the general public accept this as customary. We expect to pay more for a product or service depending upon which market we opt to shop in. It's no different for mobile DJs except for the very fact that we are 'mobile' which means that we can take our product or service into many different markets.

Usually a product or a service will be priced according to supply and demand. Rolls-Royce doesn't make as many cars as Ford. However, Rolls-Royce doesn't sell cars for $20,000 nor does Ford sell cars for $1,000,000. If I wanted to send a parcel to Florida I could take it to the post office and wait in line to be served. They would weigh it and I would pay them maybe $15 to cover the cost of shipping. Then I would make my way back home. Alternatively, I could go online and use the internet to find an international mail company like DHL who will come to my home and collect the parcel and deliver it to Florida for $50.

I now have a choice. I can elect to pay more for the convenience and service provided by DHL who do the work for me or I can pay less for an inferior service.

There are over 3,500 legal mobile DJs in Australia (IBISWorld); many of these DJs believe that they can't charge more than $500 for a night's work. However, a minority of quality, talented mobile DJs in Australia regularly earn upwards of $1200 for a night's work. I would also wager there is a group of DJs who have no problem earning in excess of $2000 for their services. And I know for a fact that in America there are mobile DJs/MCs whose fee is over $5000. Unfortunately we seldom hear about these successful businessmen and women. Most of us are deafened by those that insist there is no money to be made as a mobile DJ. The sad fact is that it is those low-priced DJs who are dragging the market down. It becomes a self-fulfilling prophecy. If you tell yourself something often enough or hear it repeated often enough you tend to believe it is true. My suggestion to you is, "Do not listen to those who say you can't. Listen to those who say you can". I would also suggest that you disassociate yourself from negative DJs and find positive, successful role models who are prepared to share their success and help you attain the rewards you deserve.

When it comes to pricing you have a choice

Do you allow the market to dictate what you charge or do you fix a price suitable for the market into which you wish to sell your product or service? This is more difficult than it appears. I know of a photographer who offered a great service and yet he struggled for business. I met him at one of the largest wedding expos in Melbourne where there were also a couple of other photographers present. They were doing really well taking bookings on the day, whereas my friend was struggling. We spoke with the other photographers and it turned out that they had been told by various consumers that they would have booked the other photographer, but didn't do so because he was too cheap! I personally have had clients say to me that they didn't want to hire a 'cheap DJ' – for this couple a cheap DJ was under $1000. Most people realise that you get what you pay for.

It may be that you decide to target one market and have one price. Or it may be that you decide to be in a number of markets and have a multiple pricing policy. There are pros and cons to both choices. Only you can decide which is best for you. Do your research and go with whatever you are comfortable with. However, there is another option. You could introduce a price range. "Our prices start from as little as $xxx". This policy allows you the flexibility to price in accordance with your clients' needs. The more they need from you the more you will need to charge them. Simple.

Firstly you need to decide if you offer a product or a service

It's probably true to say that because of the way mobile DJs have advertised themselves over the years, the general public view what we offer as a product. Why else would they ring and ask, "How much for a DJ?" They see us as speakers, lights and music. They shop around for the best price just as if we were a tin of baked beans on a supermarket shelf. You can't blame them for this. If they can't appreciate that the difference between mobile DJs is YOU, the disc jockey, then what else are they to believe? It is our responsibility to educate the public so that they understand that it is you, the DJ, the entertainer, the expert, the experienced, and the talented professional who defines the difference between average and exceptional. Average is cheap; exceptional is priceless. So our challenge is to realise that we offer a SERVICE and that the equipment which we use is merely the tools which enable us to provide that service. The good news is this. Service is less price sensitive than a product. The bad news is, it's more difficult to sell. Or is it? Hold that thought; we'll come back to it later.

There are weddings and there are weddings. Large weddings and small weddings, some weddings are quiet, low-key affairs while others are all singing and dancing with no expense spared. And there are, of course, all kinds of weddings in-between. Basically, no two weddings are ever the same. Your challenge is to identify which weddings you want to be the DJ for.

First of all, this is not an exact science and there will always be exceptions to the rule; however, what follows is my understanding of weddings based upon my experience of providing DJ services for hundreds, if not thousands, of these events over the last 25 years. Much of what will follow has been gathered from many sources. Where possible I will give accreditation to those I have learnt from. Some of the following information is generic and impossible to trace the origin of. A list of acknowledgments and recommended reading can be found at the back of this publication.

Targeting a particular sector of the market will help you fine-tune what you do and how you communicate with potential clients. In order to do this you need to understand the market.

The market place for weddings is by its very nature diverse. In order to be effective you will need to start thinking like your client. Where do they hang out? What sort of occupation do they have? Where do they work?

Where are they likely to get married: in church or in a hotel or maybe abroad on a beach? Maybe at a registry office in town, or on the lawn of a stately manor house.

Initially, the first factor which will determine which market place you will find your ideal client will be based on the client's budget. Generally, if the budget is low then so too will be the amount they are prepared to spend on entertainment. I have been hired by a bride in the past who had a very low budget but she was prepared to pay my fee because she valued what I did; however, this is very much the exception to the rule.

How much should clients be expecting to pay for wedding entertainment? A quick search around the World Wide Web will leave you bemused and confused but it is fair to say that generally anything between five and fifteen percent of the budget should go on entertainment. This includes harpists, string quartets, Toastmasters, magicians, chocolate fountains, DJs and bands, so be careful when you do the maths or ask the question.

The average cost of a wedding in Australia (2013) is around $54,294 (according to Bride To Be magazine). This includes the honeymoon and so roughly speaking you should expect a client to be budgeting anywhere between $2,500 and $8,000 for entertainment. Further research indicates that seven and a half percent of the budget, $4,000, is a reasonable sum to work with. I know, it's a bit of a shock, isn't it? The challenge we have as DJs is to ensure we get our fair share.

In the list of other service providers there are many instances where a DJ can provide his services as a substitute which will be an opportunity to earn more money. Many clients have no idea that a DJ would be prepared to play harp or classical recordings or background music at a very low volume for a drinks reception.

You may have heard the expression that 'perception is reality'. Unfortunately in today's modern age the perception of a mobile DJ can be far from reality. This brings me to an important point which is worth remembering.

The word or term 'mobile disc jockey' no longer reflects what most of us do or how we do it. If clients see us as baseball-hat-wearing, jean-clad DJs playing house music at knee-breaking volume then that is what they will expect. I wear a tuxedo to my weddings, use very little 'in your face' lighting and play their guests' requests at a volume that does not make their ears bleed.

You could call yourself a 'presenter' or 'entertainer' or 'planner' but again you would be faced with the challenge of explaining what you do, so I guess DJ is as good as any description for the moment. The one thing this dilemma does is give you ammunition for requesting a meeting with your client prior to quoting any prices.

This is your 'way in' to explain what you do and that wedding entertainment is so much more than just music.

I digress – back to identifying your target market. I should also point out that you really need to be comfortable with your chosen market. If you are at ease in local clubs and prefer not to use the microphone then clearly you do not want to target five-star hotels where the management may expect you to make all of the announcements and introductions. I know many DJs who work in clubs who make a living from their services, just not the kind of money which they could make if they switched markets.

So, logically, the more that is being spent on the wedding the more potential you have of earning a realistic fee; note I use the word 'earning'. This is not just a case of charging more for the same service provided the night before at a birthday party. If you buy into the concept of providing a more personal and tailored service then you will need to spend more time with your client prior to the event in order to explore their vision and turn their dreams into reality. More about that later in the book.

You may be apprehensive about asking about clients' budgets on the phone or at an initial meeting, so how do you gauge the situation? Generally the first hint will come from the choice of venue. Do your research and check out how much local hotels charge for wedding receptions. How much is a typical cost 'per head' for a wedding at that five-star hotel in the city? Also enquire how much a marquee would cost to hire and then add the price for caterers. You will be amazed at how much even simple things like a glass of wine costs at some venues.

The other thing you need to remember about weddings is that often logic and rationale go out of the window. Human beings often act in strange ways. Remember we talked about perception often being reality. Well, some people, especially the father of a bride, will subscribe to this rationale: "nothing is too much trouble and no expense will be spared" in order to achieve what he wants for his daughter. Remember too that you cannot judge a book by its cover or, even worse, judge people by your own standards.

Some mobile DJs have a problem often referred to as 'a poverty mentality'. This relates to them not being able to understand why someone would want to pay five dollars each for nothing more than a few coloured lollies wrapped up in a fancy bag with a guest's name on the outside. Five times 100 guests is $500 for favours, yet he doesn't believe he can get more than $500 for his DJ services? Sometimes we are our own worst enemies.

Nimby? Or, not in my back yard

I am indebted to Randy Bartlett, an exceptionally talented DJ, who explained this misnomer to me a few years back. I shall try to explain it to you. Some DJs believe that there is no way on earth they could realise $750 or $1500 for their DJ services where they live. I have heard this argument time and time again as I have travelled around the country attending meetings of DJ associations. Invariably they will cite local unemployment, the economy and other DJs who persistently quote $200 or less for a 'DJ'. They are also quick to point out that it would be easy to get $750 or $1500 in posh places or capital cities.

The reality is that there are clients in every community who are prepared to pay more for quality products and services regardless of their perceived social status. Just take a walk down any road in a council estate and look at the cars parked outside the homes. Logic would dictate that they would all be old battered vehicles which had seen better days or small economical cars that were at the lower end of the price range. Reality is a different story. You will see all of the abovementioned cars but you will also see new ones, big ones and often more expensive ones than you can afford to drive. We have no way of knowing those people's circumstances. They may choose to spend their cash on cars rather than smokes or booze. They could have won the car in a competition or it could be a company car. All we know is that in any market there is a need. The difference is that the market may be bigger or smaller depending on where you live.

Every community has professional people working and living in the area: doctors, solicitors, architects, bankers, dentists – the list is endless. Where do they go to eat, drink and relax? Restaurants, golf clubs and quality hotels are where you will find them. DJs like Steve Bowen in Albury, NSW, Mark Wall and Adam Scott in Ballarat, Victoria, Mark Weller in South Wales, Brian Mole in the south east and Alan Marshall in the south central part of England, together with dozens more who maintain a lower profile, are living proof that you can earn good money by providing personalised, professional DJ services anywhere in the country.

Do you want to be a big fish in a small pond?
Or a little fish in a large pond?

Too often we chase the wrong market and find it hard to make an impact. There may be strong competition and it's difficult to get your company recognised among all the other adverts in yellow pages or your website to the top of the Google rankings. It is much more sensible to look for a niche market and make it your own. Think outside of the box and use innovative methods to get your name or brand recognised.

What's in a name?

If you are targeting the high-end wedding market you need to give a great deal of thought about what you call yourself or your business. 'Dave Double Decks' or 'Celebration Discos' or 'Stayin' Alive' or 'Party Hard' does not exactly fill me with confidence that you are a specialist wedding professional. Quite the contrary; these names suggest cheesy 70s or 80s Smashy and Nicey DJs. Which also brings me to another point …

Do clients want a DJ or a disco? How do you view yourself? Are you a mobile discothèque or are you the DJ, the entertainer? I would suggest that many of those cheesy names of old are from a time gone by when indeed people used to look for a 'disco'. Today a modern bride will be looking for an entertainer. Yes, you still need the equipment but today this equipment is smaller and less in your face. Brides are more interested in the 'look' of a room and the last thing they want is loads of sound and lighting equipment taking up the entire dance floor. Or worse, detracting from the overall look of the room she has spent a small fortune on to look elegant.

My advice would be to rebrand. Choose a name which reflects you and your services. Keep it simple. It may be something like 'Mark Jones, Wedding DJ'. Alternatively, you may want to have a business name like 'Elegant Wedding DJ Services'. Either way, try to use the words to describe who you are and what you do.

Over in America there is a very successful and talented mobile DJ called Peter Merry. His company is called 'Merry Weddings'; he has also rebranded himself as a 'Wedding Entertainment Director'. I know he earns top dollar for all of his services and rightly so. You will find more information about Peter at the rear of the book.

Product focused or service focused?

Peter was the first person to show me the distinction between viewing my company as a product or service. Let me ask you the same question: are you product focused or service focused?

Take a look at your business cards, website and flyers. Do they feature lots of pictures of equipment? If so, why?

Would you go along to a building contractor when looking for him to build you an extension and ask him, "What kind of cement mixer do you use"? You would be more interested to see an example of his finished work or testimonials from satisfied customers. Quality equipment is vital for us to use as professionals. We appreciate its reliability and the cool things it helps us do but your client couldn't give a flying fig.

There is an equation which may help you understand the way that markets work and what it takes to target a particular market. Any business will strive to offer these three things: low cost, great service, high quality.

In reality you can only provide two out of the three.

Low cost and great service is fine but the quality will suffer. Great service and high quality are fine but will not be offered at low cost. High quality and low cost will not be delivered by great service.

Apply this model to any successful business you can think of. Whilst they will strive to achieve all three the reality is that only two can be delivered consistently. This is why companies target markets and concentrate on their two strongest traits whilst accepting the third as the price paid for the success of the company.

A bride and groom are looking for someone who cares about the success of their wedding reception. They want someone they respect and trust to represent them on their big day. They expect you to have the tools required to do the job.

They trust you will deliver great music and interaction on their behalf in a way which reflects their personalities in a style they are comfortable with. Most importantly of all, they want peace of mind. They need to know that you will deliver exactly what you promised.

Getting started

Targeted marketing is all about doing lots of little things directed at people and places where your ideal client is most likely to be. In order to be successful targeted marketing needs to be personal. You need to think like a bride and groom. It helps if you are married yourself as this goes someway to having an empathy with your prospective client.

Your business card
You only get one chance to make a first impression.

Please, please, please do not design and print your own cards at home. Do not cut them out and laminate them. Do not use one of those online companies who print them but leave their advertising on the back. These entire things say only one thing about you: CHEAP!

If you expect your customers to view you as a quality professional mobile DJ then please use your marketing materials to reflect this. Therefore you need to employ an expert to help transform your brand or image into one that gets across the right message. The card should feel good when passed between the fingers. Alternatively the card may be of a unique material or shape. What you should be aiming for is that your card would stand out if pinned to a notice board among fifty other DJs' business cards.

The same thinking should be applied to all of your marketing materials. Try and be different. As well as flyers or brochures think about key rings, branded pens or mugs. The best branded promotional material I found was a desk notepad. Imagine having your company details on a desk in front of event managers and wedding planners every time they sat at their desk. In addition to your contact details I would have this year and next year's calendar details on the pad thereby making it practical and useful.

If you want to be seen as a quality 'DJ' then everything you do should reflect that. Not just stationery: what you wear on your wrist, your aftershave to the car you drive – how often do you wash your car? You would be surprised at what some brides will notice.

Wedding expos

They are the most obvious example of targeted marketing. After all, people visiting a wedding expo are basically admitting they need help and assistance in turning their vision into reality. However, I must issue a health warning here: *people don't know what they don't know.*

That is to say, they may have an idea of what they want but they have absolutely no idea as to how to make it happen. How many times have I heard a bride say to me that she wanted everybody to join her on the dance floor after her first dance?

"So how are we going to achieve that?" I would teasingly reply. "Play a really modern piece of music which everyone will know," she would reply. It's at this point when tact and diplomacy come into play because you and I know that this is easier said than done. More about this topic in the 'staging' section of the book.

When it comes to wedding expos you need to be aware of hidden agendas. Some are promoted by specialist companies and to them is an event to make money, period. They will not limit the number of exhibitors in any category and they have no ongoing relationship with the venue. Other specialist companies promote the hotel and only invite existing service providers endorsed by the venue or others where the venue has no preferred supplier.

Finally there are events organised by the venue itself. These can vary from a closed shop to an open house. My advice to you is to do your research and check out exactly what the situation is with regard to mobile DJs. In other words, does the venue policy limit your opportunities to do business with the visitors? Being prepared will enable you to target visitors to your table / booth accordingly and also enable you to make a value decision as to whether this is a viable form of marketing for you.

"Wedding expos are a waste of time," one prominent DJ who shall remain nameless once said to me. To which I replied, "It's how you approach them that makes all the difference."

Let me explain. You should not expect a bride and groom to visit your stand / booth, chat for a couple of minutes and then say "Yes". Realistically the best you can hope for is that they agree to take your information and allow you to contact them so that you may discuss their requirements.

If you consider the time constraints and the practical and logistical issues with trying to sell your services whilst others are milling around, and no doubt noisy distractions from other vendors going on all around you, it is much better to be short and sweet and to the point.

Introduce yourself, give a brief outline of who you are and what you do and then hit them with a reason why they should employ you.

Leave them wanting to know more and you are halfway there to setting up a meeting. Less is best, and a wedding expo is no exception. Don't take along your full set-up and spread it across the back wall of the venue. Ideally don't take your equipment at all, unless you are asked to provide background music or music for a fashion show.

Brides and grooms are not impressed by your equipment: only other DJs are. If you feel the need to flaunt your latest purchase then use a photograph or better still record a video and show it on your iPad or monitor screen.

Less is best: Dress your booth in such a way as to invite people in and ask what it is you do? Be engaging; show a genuine interest in your potential client. Demonstrate that you care about their big day and offer advice. Personally all I take to an expo is a big screen TV and I play videos from weddings I have performed at, and because I don't have any DJ gear a lot of people think I'm a videographer, until they get closer; once they realise I'm a DJ, well, let's just say it's a good ice breaker.

Remember, people buy people.

Most cost-effective way of attending wedding expos?

If you can negotiate a contra-invoice deal where they charge you for your stand / booth and you charge them for hosting the bridal fashion show you get a win-win outcome. Firstly it costs you nothing more than your time. Secondly it gives you the opportunity to be the MC at the event. This works on so many levels it's unbelievable. Visitors will be able to hear your voice on the microphone and get a snapshot of your style of presentation. They will hear the quality of your sound system. You will also get a chance to network with other wedding vendors who will want you to promote their services before, during and after the fashion show.

More importantly it is a fantastic platform for you to present your opening info-commercial at the beginning of the show. I always used to open my introduction by asking all the brides in the audience to raise their hands, or stand up, so that we, the remaining people in the audience and the vendors, got a good look at their potential customers. I would engage them in conversation by asking how they were feeling and what it was they wanted to get out of the expo today. What services were they looking for, etc. At the end of the show my final words would be an invitation to come and join me at my stand if they needed information about great wedding entertainment.

Specialist bridal magazines and venue brochures

Warning! Print advertising can be expensive. However, if you are targeting a specific geographical area or a particular venue it can be very effective. Just be careful and do your research. Some DJs swear by advertising in upmarket publications.
You know, the kind of publication which advertises homes for sale valued at millions of dollars and features glossy photo shoots of the latest watches priced at $30,000.

Take my advice and use a professional agency to design your advertisement. Their expertise will help you get results. Venue brochures can also be a prime source for your advertising. They are handed to all prospective clients by the venue and will therefore reach your targeted brides regardless of whether or not they book that particular venue. If you happen to be the preferred supplier to that venue then so much the better: it's a double whammy. A word of warning here. In some instances these brochures are produced by a third party company who have no connection with the venue other than to promote the venue itself. Therefore they have no regard for the advertisers and the venue has no commitment to use them as preferred suppliers. In addition to this I have known venues to be sold or rebranded after a short period resulting in the brochure being discarded, leaving advertisers badly out of pocket. Proceed with caution and do your research before committing to what is often a one- or two-year contract.

Social networking sites

These sites are becoming more and more accessible to potential clients. The social demographics of these places make targeted marketing easier. If you promote your business on these sites you will find it easier to 'connect' and keep people informed instantaneously as to who you are and what you are doing. I am no expert so I would again urge you to take professional assistance when placing your company on one of these sites. I would suggest that you do keep your personal information separate from your business profile. All too often I see DJs promoting how professional they are only to find them using inappropriate language and discussing less tasteful issues for all to see. Not a good idea.

Your website can be fine-tuned or targeted

A page of your website or better still an entirely separate website should be directed toward the wedding market. The content should be about helping brides and grooms, offering advice and showing images of other happy couples who have used your services. It should be crammed with testimonials. It should also encourage visitors to get in touch with you to arrange a meeting. Include a recent photograph or two of yourself. Provide information with regard to your location and list high-end venues where you have performed.

Do not copy any material from a website. Respect copyright and your fellow DJs' intellectual property.

You don't need to cram every tiny detail into your website. These days it is easy to believe that a website is the answer to all of our dreams. Some believe that an all singing and dancing website will do everything. It will attract customers who will use all of the interactive tools and then they can select their package, pay online and print off their contract – brilliant! Except that not everyone wants to buy a service this way – products maybe, but not a service. Service requires a human interface. The problem with relying on their input is that you only get to know what they choose to tell you.

Why meet with your potential client?

Because just like them, and here's the shocker,

"You don't know what you don't know."

How many times have you quoted a price only to hear the person on the other end of the phone say, "Oh, is that all, I thought it would be more than that." Or maybe you have quoted a price and turned up at the venue only to find that there are stilt walkers, fire eaters, chocolate fountains, casino tables, free bar, magicians wandering around, a comedian working with you as well as a thirteen-piece band and you know, you just know, that you are the lowest paid of them all!

Here's something else to think about. In the sales process very few people buy at the first point of contact. This would be an impulse buy and very few brides will book their wedding DJ based on an impulse. Generally we all need to have several points of contact with a product or service before we are happy to buy.

Having made a decision, especially to purchase something expensive, we then seek reassurance that we have made the right decision. So it is unrealistic, from the outset, to expect a client to make a decision based on a visit to a website or a phone call.

It is much better for all involved to meet and spend time exploring each other's wants and needs. It's fascinating just how much more information is revealed over a nice cup of coffee. More on this topic later.

Time invested

It's a widely recognised fact in sales training that the more time you spend with a potential customer the more likely they are to buy from you. The longer you spend listening to their needs and responding with useful and practical examples of how you can fit in with their requirements and provide what they want, the more chance they will hire you.

If you get agreement along the way the customer is mentally assuming that you are already working for them. If they present objections and you are able to overcome them and demonstrate the benefits of using your services then gradually the sales resistance is lowered.

Finally, if you are able to convince them that what you offer cannot be found elsewhere and that you represent excellent value, you will have removed any competition and they will be happy to hire you.

Quality venues

There is no substitute for meeting face to face with clients. Gaining access to them is the hard part. Many clients can be found at upmarket venues; however, it may be the venue management who are instrumental when it comes to choice of entertainment. They may not have a resident DJ but opt to have a list of preferred suppliers. This can be a good thing and a not-so-good thing. You need to know what the criteria are for being placed on the list. I would recommend you set up a meeting with the event coordinator to explore the possibility of you becoming a preferred supplier. If the venue is interested in professionalism and entertainment all should be fine. If, however, they are more interested in how much money you are prepared to pay for a referral or booking proceed with caution.

3] HANDLING ENQUIRIES

By telephone

The telephone enquiry is probably still the most important method of communication for businesses. You can gauge so much from the way a telephone call is handled, both good and bad.

How you answer the phone speaks volumes about your professed professionalism. You need to answer the phone within the first four or five rings or risk the caller hanging up. Answer in a clear, calm and collected way stating who you are and the name of your company followed by, "How can I help you"? Have a list of questions prepared which you will need to ask in order to get as full a picture as possible of the caller's requirements. It's a good idea to have a specific 'enquiry pad' located by the phone or in your car. See the example below.

Invariably the 'how much' question will be asked, often as the opening line. Be prepared and have your answers ready. Remember you don't actually need to answer this question directly. There are many methods of 'deflecting' the price issue until either you are ready to give an approximate quotation or better still to explain that your services "start from $xxx to $yyy and I'm sure we can tailor a package to suit your budget".

Ideally, because you are selling a service, or range of services, it is better to steer the conversation toward the meeting from the outset. It may be that your marketing materials say, "Call us today to arrange a free, no-obligation meeting". This makes things so much easier. I know of many DJs who make it plain on their website that pricing will not be disclosed over the phone or via email.

Whilst on the subject of phone calls here are a few things to bear in mind:

1] Have a dedicated phone for your DJ business or at least a number which has a different ring tone so that whenever a client calls you know it is a business call and you can answer in the appropriate manner.

2] Never allow anyone other than yourself or partner / employee answer the business call. The last thing you want is a child to answer and then to have to shout for you to take the call.

3] If you can't answer the phone for whatever reason try to have the call redirected to someone who can take it for you.

There are professional companies who will do this for not a lot of money. Remember, one call successfully converted could pay for their services. A missed call could be a lost customer.

4] As a last resort have your calls routed to voicemail. A clear business-like message and a promise to return the call is all that is needed. Check your messages regularly and return calls as quickly as possible.

Here's something to consider

You may be a great DJ but that doesn't mean you have the skills for telephone sales. It is sometimes good to know your limitations and use the talents of others to do this part of the business for you. It's also another great way of setting up a meeting so that your telephone operator can fill your diary. I would also suggest that in this particular market most of the calls are made by women.

Usually it is the bride herself, sometimes a friend or maybe her mother. If the incoming enquiry is handled by a woman there is almost an instant empathy. Women love to talk, especially about weddings and all that goes with them. Once engaged in conversation and demonstrating a genuine care for the caller, and her big day, sales resistance is lowered. People buy people and if you can get on the same wavelength it's amazing how this will positively affect how they perceive you and your business.

First-time caller?

People do not tend to book DJs very often unless they are corporate clients, agencies or wedding planners. It is a good idea once you have answered the call and introduced yourself to ask who is calling.
A bride will have very little experience, if any, of booking a DJ so it is no surprise that the first question will be either about your availability or price; this is because she will not know what else to ask by way of opening the conversation.

Asking "Where did you hear about me / us?" is a great question to ask a caller. The reply will determine how you proceed with the call. It may be that she has seen you before and picked up your card either directly from you or a friend. In this situation you can refer to that event and ask more questions. It may be that she has seen your advertisement in yellow pages.

"Are we the first DJ service you have rung?" The answer to this will also give you a couple of options. If she says yes, ask why.

What was it about your advert which prompted her to call? It may be that she has tried other numbers but you were the only person to answer. What does that tell you about your competition? More importantly, if the caller admits to ringing other DJs you need to find out why she is still calling other DJs. What is it that she is looking for that she has not found elsewhere? It may be that she is shopping the world for the best (lowest) price or it may be that she just hasn't been able to find someone she likes and trusts. Someone she is comfortable with.

If the caller has never booked a DJ before she will probably have no idea with regard to the range of services on offer or the standards of equipment and performance skills which are available. At this point she thinks a DJ is just music and lights and that DJs are pretty much the same. She wants a price but she doesn't know what she will get in return. She needs help. She is probably confused but doesn't want to admit it; if you ask the right questions you can find out her fears and why she's confused, because a confused mind says no!

Imagine a woman ringing up Harvey Norman and asking, "Do you sell TVs, I'd like to buy a TV, how much are your TVs?" They would reply, "We have many TVs in many different sizes and quality. They range from $160 to $25, 000; which would you prefer?" In reality the woman would quickly realise that she needed to visit the store and get some expert advice on what to buy. This is typical when people buy a product but we do not offer products, we supply a service. What we sell is invisible, which makes the whole process more difficult … for some.

Pricing

I suggest you do not give a specific price in the first 30 seconds, if at all. Once they have their price, chances are they will only be half listening to what you say after that.

Deflect the price question with general but truthful replies such as:

"Less than you would expect for the quality we deliver."

"We tailor our pricing to your requirements; please tell me more about …"

"It really does depend on what you require us to do; can I ask you …"

"Our services range from $750 to $3995 for each event; how long do you need the DJ for?"

"We have several packages which may suit your requirements; let's see if we can find the right one for you."

Sometimes callers insist on a price and you have to give it. Be confident and tell them. After you give the price there are a few options as to what you do or say next. Once you have quoted your price … shut up, say nothing. Do not try to justify it. Leave it. Wait for the caller to reply. Sometimes there may be a stony silence. Fine. Generally the next person to speak has lost. If you speak first the sale is lost or at best you will be going over old ground. If the caller speaks it will either be to confirm she has understood or needs more information. She may well want clarification or have more questions or she may raise an objection. Remember this, sometimes an objection is not a "No", it's "I need more information or I haven't been convinced as to your value yet".

Or you could simply ask the question, "How does that sound?" after you have given the price. This keeps the conversation flowing and doesn't give them enough time to really think about asking you more questions to justify the price. They might say, "This is more than I expected." You could reply with, "Really? What did you think it was worth?" And then it might become a conversation about helping or educating the client. Maybe you could suggest that, "Most people prefer to meet me so they have a better understanding of how I can help them"; even better they might say, "Is that all?" Own the fact you charge what you charge.

Reassure

Do not talk technical stuff. Use simple words and be confident and competent. Use phrases like "No problem", or "We can do that", or "More than happy" and "We can take care of that for you".

Finally

Just ask for the business. "Can we book it for you?", or "Should I pencil you in?", or "Can I go ahead and reserve that date for you?"

Or more positive sales closing lines like, "Would you like the silver package or the gold?" or "Would you like to pay the initial payment by cheque or with a card?"

If all else fails: "Can I send you some information through the post for you to take a look at?"

Price objections – "I can get a DJ for $300"

I love that objection. I would answer with, "Why haven't you booked them then?" (with my tongue firmly in my cheek). Whatever you do, don't start putting the competition down; making someone else look bad doesn't make you look good. Challenge the client to wonder why another DJ is offering such a low price.

A] Is he a registered business? Do they have public liability insurance?

B] Will they secure the booking with a written contract?

C] Can he provide references from previous clients and venues?

D] Has he explained what happens if he is ill or unable to perform?

E] Is price more important to you than your guests' enjoyment and satisfaction?

F] Would you rather have an average DJ at an average price or a specialist for a fair price?

G] My phone is always ringing off the hook on a weekend with people whose $300 DJs have failed to show up!

H] I can give you the contact details for dozens of DJs who charge $300 but I wouldn't recommend them or send them to one of our clients.

I] Has he undertaken any DJ/MC-related workshops or been to any training courses in the last two years?

J] Does he have some examples of his work? (video or audio recordings)

K] So why are you ringing me?

I'm sure you could easily come up with several other questions, not that you will ask them all; once you find out more details and find out their fears you'll be able to ask the appropriate questions and give the answers to show that you are an expert.

Handling email enquiries

I must admit to not being a lover of email enquiries particularly those which ask for a price but have no other contact information. You often end up playing email tag and getting nowhere fast. However, sometimes you need to take control and explain how you feel and lay down your terms with regard to giving prices without all the information you require.

Here are some ideas as to how to tackle this thorny issue.

Ron Michaels, a fellow DJ, believes in pre-qualifying contacts and has this on his web site:

INITIAL CONSULTATION REQUIRED ...
Please be advised that I don't quote prices on the phone or email. An initial consultation is required for all potential clients. There is no way I can explain the unique services I offer, get a true sense of what your needs and expectations are, or see if we are going to be a good fit for each other in a 10-minute phone call.

However, he does go on to say:

PRICING & PACKAGES...
Prices vary depending on the services you need and the time commitment required. Packages start at $600. >

I found that the following two ideas often worked well.

You may want to go down the path of reasoning

"Dear client, choosing your DJ service should be a two-way process. Your DJ needs to understand your vision of how your perfect day will unravel and be remembered as a truly unforgettable day.

Any DJ who quotes you an average fee without meeting with you and exploring your needs is doing you and your guests a disservice. If he is not prepared to invest time in researching your needs and then explaining how he can make your wedding reception fun, unique and memorable, as I can, he will only deliver an 'average' performance.

Do you want an 'average' wedding reception or one tailor-made which will reflect your personalities and be conducted in the 'style' of your choice? Give me a call on 01234 567896 and let's get together for a no-obligation chat over a cup of coffee."

You could also go down the comparison route

"Choosing a DJ service is just like hiring a photographer, vintage car company, cake maker or hairdresser. You need to be able to make a 'value' decision based on not only what I do but 'how' I do it. A fantastic and memorable wedding reception doesn't just 'happen'. It needs to be planned and managed.

You probably have many questions to ask; indeed, I have many questions to ask you and would welcome the opportunity to explain the whole process and the costs for my services. Quality isn't expensive ... it's priceless!

I'll buy the coffee; where should we meet up? How about the hotel on Wednesday evening?"

Many of you may know Richard Mills. He is a very talented DJ from New Zealand. This is how Richard tackles the issue on his website and blog.

Check out Richard Mills' blog on the subject.

Open letter to couples just looking for a price for a DJ
By DJ Richard Mills www.awardentertainment.co.nz

I've had a spate of enquiries lately from couples wanting a quote before talking or meeting with me. I find this very difficult because my service isn't a 'five hours' type of service by any measure. I'm often on site from a couple of hours before the ceremony until half an hour after the finish of the reception. Fourteen-hour days aren't uncommon. Price isn't an easy thing to discuss without an understanding of value.

This is, of course, after I've already done the 12 to 20 hours of preparation, which includes planning, run-sheet creation, communication with other vendors, correspondence, meetings, phone calls, emails, music acquisition, scripting, rehearsal, training and of course equipment maintenance.

Communicating this well in an email is impossible. Over the phone it's possible but difficult. In a meeting, couples start to really 'get it' and start to see the importance of the entertainment as a considerable percentage of the overall success of the wedding day. Once they see that percentage, the percentage of the overall wedding day budget starts to make sense and my service becomes a very viable investment.

A bride once told me that she was going to get 150 quality chair covers with beautiful sashes at $18 each. She had originally budgeted $2700 for things that, *although beautiful, were going to be under her guests' backsides for much of the reception. After our consultation, priorities changed dramatically and her DJ budget tripled. Their wedding was stunning and their guests are still talking about it two years later. I know, because some of them have now booked me for their weddings. Here then, is my open letter to couples who want a quote from me before talking with me about what I can do for them and their guests.*

Thank you for your enquiry. I hope the following comes across the right way – the written word is so difficult.

I'm not cheap, and there are a lot of reasons for that. In fact, I'm one of the most expensive wedding DJs in the country, and I usually work around 30 weddings per year at prices at the very top of the range in New Zealand. For that rate, my clients get a totally unique and personalised service and I'm booked on referrals almost exclusively.

People hire me to ensure that their wedding will be unlike any other celebration that they and their guests have ever been to. They book me to ensure that their day flows perfectly, that their guests don't leave as soon as the DJ starts and that everyone feels like they are part of something truly special and memorable.

Typically I put between 12 and 20 hours of preparation into every wedding, plus 12 or 14 hours on site on the day. If you really just want three and a half hours of music, I'm not the DJ for you and you'll likely find a 'turn up and press play' DJ for around a quarter of my fee.

If you want some ideas to help make your day one that your guests will talk about happily for years to come, then we should talk.

Regards,
Richard Mills
Winner Best Nationwide DJs & MCs, Corporate Events Guide People's Choice Awards

For the record, personalised wedding entertainment with Richard ranges in price depending on many factors including location, but is typically between $2800 and $5000.

Whichever way you choose to deal with enquiries you should strive to be comfortable, relaxed and confident. Like all things in this book:

"It's not what you do, it's the way that you do it that gets results."

4] ITS NOT WHAT YOU DO ...

Creating great entertainment is all about how you approach what you are doing and understanding that on this occasion it's not about you, it's about your clients: the bride and groom.

Everything you do should be representative of them and portrayed in the style they are comfortable with. This means that you have a responsibility to deliver slightly different performances each time you undertake a task. Let's take a look at the kind of opportunities you have as a DJ to enhance what may otherwise be an 'average' part of a bride and groom's big day. In all of the following scenarios I will illustrate what often happens at a 'typical' event and then I will suggest a better, more personalised vision of how you can make it a better experience for the happy couple.

Civil ceremony

All too frequently, in my opinion, it seems that a civil ceremony is little more than a business transaction: signed, sealed and delivered in no time at all. I once attended a family member's wedding at a stylish hotel. We arrived in good time and were herded into the bar and encouraged to have a drink. The wedding was due to take place at 2.30 and just after 2.20 I noticed that everyone was still in the bar chatting and drinking. At 2.25 on the dot a member of the hotel staff announced that we were to make our way to the suite for the wedding ceremony. All drinks had to be abandoned because they are not allowed in the room where the registrar has authority.

We all piled in, grabbed our seats, and within no time at all the bride was walking up the 'aisle'. I had been aware of some kind of 'muzak' being played as we entered the room but there had not been a discernible change or increased volume to announce the arrival of the bride other than the registrar's instruction that we should all stand.

The ceremony began. The formalities were completed, vows exchanged and the rings presented to their respective fingers and there you had it: "Husband and wife, you may kiss the bride". They signed the register, had a few photos taken and then they proceeded back through the congregation and we were invited to join the happy couple in the bar. Surely there must be a better way. There is!

Picture this. A professional sound system and DJ positioned discreetly in the room where the wedding is to take place.

This time there is a DJ who understands that he is not allowed to speak until after the wedding ceremony. This guy has a plan up his sleeve. This DJ has explained to his client that by doing things a little differently the occasion will take on more meaning and be a memorable experience for both them and their guests.

Let's begin with seating the guests; would it not be better for them to be shown into the room earlier and for them to be ushered to their seats? While this is going on how about we play music selected by the groom? This music will be his opportunity to send a message, through his music choice, which will create the atmosphere for what is about to happen. It will also enable the groom to relax while he is waiting for the arrival of his bride. There will be a secret signal, shared only by the bride and groom, which will indicate that the bride is about to enter the room. This 'secret' will be a special piece of music, which when played will tell the groom that his wife-to-be is here and that she is about to enter the room. The next piece of music to be played will be the bride's choice. This music is her 'entrance' and the one to which she will walk up the 'aisle' after the registrar has asked the congregation to stand. The volume levels will rise and fall at the appropriate time to add dynamics to the event and will have been agreed with the registrar beforehand. All it takes is eye contact and coordination.

Our DJ will have asked his client about suitable music for the time when the register is signed. Once again volume levels can rise and add emotion to the proceedings. Once the formalities are completed and the volume again is lowered to allow the registrar to say a few final words of congratulations and the inevitable "Please stand", the final rousing 'recession' music can be played. This choice may be traditional or something wacky. I would encourage clients to go with their hearts and select something which makes a statement about them. It is, after all is said and done, their big day.

Now, and only now, can the DJ speak and, as usual, less is more. Keep it short and sweet, along the lines of "Mr and Mrs Williams would like to invite everyone to join them outside in the garden for drinks and photographs." Job done, but in a much more personal and emotional way!

Empower your clients

When you explain what you can do to help them create a unique and personal experience the end result is only limited by imagination. I had one groom who selected six tracks all written by The Beatles.

Of course, all his family knew he was a fan so it came as no surprise to hear his favourite music whilst they waited for the bride to arrive. Songs like 'And I love her' and 'Something' made an instant connection with those present and took on a whole new meaning as part of a wedding ceremony.

On another occasion a couple who had been together for a number of years before deciding to marry decided on a Walt Disney theme. 'One day my prince will come' and 'The meaning of life', not forgetting 'Beauty and the beast', were all featured. The guests didn't know whether to laugh or cry. They ended up doing both at various parts of the ceremony.

Receiving lines – why do them?

If you ask a bride and groom if they are having a receiving line, most will not know what one is or will have been told not to bother with one because they take too much time to arrange and will delay the start of the wedding meal. Usually this 'advice' is given by the venue management because all they are interested in is getting the food served as quickly as possible. This stinks of the tail wagging the dog again.

A receiving line can be a great way to help seat guests and also give the bride and groom an opportunity to say hello to their guests. You need to explain to them that after their wedding ceremony there is a good chance that the next hour or so will be spent having photographs taken and they will have little chance to spend time with their guests. If they are not careful the management will expect them to be seated and served with food without a chance to meet their guests and relax. Therefore a receiving line can work on two levels. First, it allows the bride and groom to briefly acknowledge their guests while also creating an orderly stream of people entering the room and finding their designated places.

This is something which you can help with. You can also take advantage of the opportunity to have another discreet sound system in the room so that you can play appropriate and customised background music. So much better than the same old CD that would probably have been the choice of the hotel staff. Either way, the bride and groom should have an informed choice. Traditionally the receiving line will consist of the entire 'bridal party' or 'head table'; however, sometimes the line will consist of just the bride and groom. The great thing about a receiving line is that it leads nicely into a grand entrance.

Grand entrance

Some venues dilute this into 'announcing the bride and groom into the room'. In many instances this responsibility is delegated to a 'duty manager' who had no formal training and has little idea as to how to speak in public. Alas, this is so often the case.

I remember one such hotel employee who had great delight in showing me the marks on the door frame created by him rapping a couple of spoons on the door jamb in order to get people's attention. He would then announce, "Ladies and gentlemen, please stand and welcome the bride and groom." No mention of their Christian names or even their married name, just a bland statement repeated at every event. What's all that about? Certainly not a way to create a unique moment to be remembered for ever. There has to be a better way and you as a DJ and now as a Master of Ceremonies can make things so much better.

A word of warning before we proceed! What follows is not as easy as it may first appear. Toastmasters go through a training process which requires paying attention to detail and practising what they do and how they do it. The same should be said of DJs who take on the responsibility of making formal announcements and the role of a MC. The word 'master' implies 'expert' and therefore you should research what it takes to be a confident and respected MC. However, the way things are you will undoubtedly be better than most hotel employees, so go for it.

Imagine having all of the guests seated and the bridal party held back out of the room. You as the DJ/MC have a bed of music playing and you introduce the guests of honour two by two into the room using their preferred choice of Christian and surname together with a reference as to who they are and how they are related to the bride and groom. Each time the music rises and falls and applause is generated by their entrance as the doors swing open in front and then close again behind them. This process is repeated until finally it is time for the bride and groom to be announced. You change the music, make your personalised announcement and they enter the room to a cacophony of music and rapturous applause.

Which way do you think your bride and groom will want to be announced into the room? Would they entrust this vital part of the day to a hotel employee, a drunken relative or a wedding professional such as you?

Dedicated music during the meal

Here we have an opportunity to show what personalised music programming is all about. With a little bit of research and consultation it is possible to produce a play list which includes all of the types of music and favourite artists of the bridal party and their guests. This will create the right kind of atmosphere conducive for a relaxing and enjoyable meal with friends and family all engaged and included. Simply because you are now playing 'their music'.

You will have gathered by now that I do not have any great faith in hotel staff to do this kind of thing. I may well be guilty of tarring them all with the same brush. There may be some out there who do a good job but to be honest 'good' doesn't cut it anymore. Bride and grooms deserve better. Some will opt for a professional Toastmaster. Fine. I just don't believe they should have to when we can do things differently. We have the advantage of using music to underscore what we do. Music evokes passion and passion is emotional. Our combination of emotional music and clear announcements should make us the preferred choice for these ceremonies. Alas, most brides do not know that we can provide these services.

Formal announcements and speeches

Here again you have an opportunity to shine. You are in the room and you have a microphone or two so extending your duties to include introducing the principal speakers is a no-brainer. Again, nothing fancy is required. Keep it simple. Less is best.

1] "Ladies and gentlemen, it is my pleasure to introduce to you the father of the bride, Mr Peter Smith."

2] "Thank you, Peter, next please welcome our groom, Mr David Skinner."

3] "Thanks, David, well done, you can relax now, or maybe not. Please welcome our best man, Mr Brian Page."

The first two announcements are very dry. No need for padding. Remember this is not about you, it's about them. Usually they will want a minimum of fuss. The third announcement is a little more relaxed and implies that the best man's speech may be, and often is, a mixture of things the groom may not want divulged to the assembled guests. The important issue here is to discuss the style in which you make the announcements with your bride and groom. For instance, they may not wish you to use the formal 'Mr'. They may prefer to have you use Christian names only. They may wish for you to make the first announcement but then want each speaker to introduce the following one in turn. Whatever works for them is fine. The important thing is that they have a choice and that you are able to facilitate that choice.

The cutting of the cake

Why do a bride and groom cut the wedding cake? Have you any idea? I believe most couples have no idea other than the fact that they are expected to have one. It is little wonder that the cake cutting is reduced to little more than a photo opportunity.

Cutting of the cake is so much more than a photo opportunity. In order to understand why and how this ceremony, for that is what it is, can contribute to a memorable moment in the day's proceedings, we need to do some research. There are many explanations depending on country of origin and certain religious beliefs. This is how I would explain the tradition and suggest a better way of using this ceremony to create more impact on the day's proceedings.

Historically the ingredients for a cake were very expensive and therefore a cake at a wedding was a symbol of prosperity. The icing would have been white and this would represent purity. The idea of sharing something so expensive and pure with your guests was considered to be a gesture which would bring good luck in return; there is also some who believe that sharing crumbs or parts of the cake has a reference to fertility.

The main significance to cutting of the cake is in relation to the fact that this is the first time the bride and groom are working together. It is their first act as husband and wife. In some instances the idea of the bride and groom cutting the cake and then actually feeding each other will symbolise that they will look out for each other and provide for each other, which, when you think about it, is exactly what marriage is all about.

So here we have a perfect opportunity not only to make the announcement aided by a great choice of music – 'Love and marriage' insert your own choice here – together with a heartfelt introduction for the bride and groom, we also have an opportunity to explain in brief why we are doing this and encourage our bride and groom to actually cut a slice and eat it.

Isn't that so much better than just a photograph of a knife plunged into a cake? I think so!

The first dance

Not all brides want to do a first dance but most will. Here again we often find that they may be shy and want little fuss. Unfortunately this can translate in some DJs' minds as to reducing this to an almost insignificant event. I often ask brides what is their experience of other weddings they may have been to.

It's amazing some of the horror stories regarding first dances. All too often it seems that little thought is given to the timing of the dance or how the introduction will be made and more importantly the logistical challenges which will affect the impact of the event.

The nightmare situation is one where the bride and groom are already on the dance floor and the DJ makes a muffled announcement which no one can understand. The dance takes place with only a few onlookers. After the dance the music changes, the bride and groom walk off the floor and the dance floor is empty.

Now I know this is an extreme example but it does happen. How do I know? Because brides have told me as much. I would hope that most DJs would have checked their sound and done a microphone test earlier in the evening. It would also help to have been given a five-minute warning so that everyone knew what was about to happen. Finally I would at least expect the DJ to have had a word with the rest of the bridal party so that they joined the bride and groom either partway through their first dance or for the next track to be played.

There has to be a better way and there is. Planning ahead and explaining how to avoid pitfalls will pay dividends later. If your bride and groom say that after their first dance they would like everyone to join them, say fine. However, we need to get everyone on board and stage manage this so that everyone knows what we expect of them. Here is a suggestion. You may have other ideas which are fine. This is something which works for me and may work for you.

You need to explain that staging and production are important and that the cooperation of the bridal party is vital to the success of the first dance and then building the dance floor. Ideally paint the picture for them. Let them envision how you would stage their first dance. Maybe you would have them stand outside the room so that you could invite them in. This would be preceded by some lively music, a fanfare or a stirring theme tune. You get everyone to stand and applaud as they enter the room and take to the floor. You introduce their first song choice and transition into the track. At the appropriate time you introduce the bridal party individually using their names. By the end of the track or the second track depending on what has been agreed you have a busy dance floor. Busy, but not full. So keeping the bridal party on the dance floor you announce that your bride and groom would like everyone to join them for the next song. This way you have a better chance of achieving your bride and groom's vision. The vision they had of a full dance floor after their first dance. Mission accomplished.

Now this is just one example of our theme "It's not what you do, it's the way that you do it that gets results." It's by no means the only way. I am sure you all have your own take on this. The important thing is that you have a structure and an idea which you share with your bride so that she understands that you care about the successful staging of her first dance. It may be that you suggest a father and daughter dance, if it's appropriate?

Many brides are not familiar with this tradition but once explained it may well be a good idea for the bride to suggest this to her father.

The father and daughter dance

It can be a nice touch to follow the bride and groom's first official dance as husband and wife with a father and daughter dance. This is when the groom steps aside and hands his wife back to 'Daddy' for one final dance. The tune to be played would be the father's choice and traditionally would carry a message of some significance. Some examples would be 'My girl' or 'I loved her first' or 'Daddy's little girl' or 'Thank heaven for little girls'; the list is endless. The beauty of this is that it brings the father into the limelight and provides a wonderful, often emotional touch to the wedding reception. Done well it will be a memorable magic moment. It can also create a bridge following the bride and groom's first dance and a more inclusive third 'family' dance with the bridal party, before you proceed to invite the rest of the guests to join you in open dance for a fourth song selection.

Another option is to have the father / daughter dance after dessert; in my experience most people will sit down to eat it. I would announce that after dessert we have another Kodak moment coming up to open the dance floor again. This is a great way to get the attention back on the dance floor and again if you stage manage it right you could ask the groom to come onto the dance floor with his mother about half way through, followed by the bridal party, and a lot of the time you won't even have to say anything as the dance floor quickly fills up again.

The buffet

Some weddings have buffet meals in the evening, some do not. Many may start late and just have one meal, others may consist of an earlier meal and a buffet later. If you have a buffet to contend with it can often be seen as dead time. Not always but often the very logistics of feeding a couple of hundred people and the timing of when the food is served can have a major impact on the evening's entertainment.

Usually it will be the venue / caterer who determines the time when food is served. This can conflict with the entertainment and restrict the choice of timing for a first dance. I urge you to question this timing very carefully and consult with all involved as to the thinking about where and when food is served. Moving the time a buffet is served forward or back by half an hour can have a big impact as to the 'flow' of the evening.

Inevitably there will be need for compromise. Keep your options open and always be on the lookout for an opportunity to help make this part of the evening more special or different.

It is always a good idea to invite the bride and groom to 'open' the buffet and be joined by the bridal party. This will send a clear message to the guests that they are invited to join the bride and groom at the buffet table and lessen the 'we don't want to go first' syndrome. It may be that you agree to 'release' guests to the buffet table by table. Many DJs will employ some kind of trivia quiz or challenge to determine which table goes next. This can be very efficient as well as entertaining and reduces the chaos often created by a free-for-all invitation.

I often use this 'dead time' to feature my USP, or unique selling point. I have an interactive routine which slots into this time zone perfectly and which also entertains the guests whilst maintaining a focus on the bride and groom. More about this later in the book.

The bouquet toss

Brides may be confused if you should suggest a bouquet toss for the evening reception party. Traditionally the bouquet is thrown or tossed outside the church or straight after the civil ceremony. These days it's normally done at the end of the night and signals the end is near. However, you don't have to wait till the end of the night; you can use this as part of the entertainment. By recreating this on the dance floor it's a great way to kick-start the dancing, especially after a lull caused by a meal.

Just like the cake cutting, there are many explanations, depending on country of origin, as to why it's done. Modern tradition says we invite all the single ladies to the dance floor and whoever catches it is the next to be married. Problem is, sometimes there's not that many single people at a wedding.

Imagine the bride on the dance floor together with all of her friends from the hen's night and as many other girls as you can muster on the night, single or married. It will produce a great photo opportunity and when coupled with the right music will enable you to transition into a full dance floor within minutes of starting up again.

It may be necessary to provide an artificial bouquet for this as many brides will not wish to throw their own. Indeed it may not be advisable when you consider how much they cost and what they are made of. I often used to have the bride pretend to throw her own bouquet only to substitute our own artificial one at the last moment. The bride does not have to throw the bouquet; brides can present the bouquet to someone special, perhaps someone who recently got engaged or to her grandmother.

Another option to throwing the bouquet is get the bride to stand in the middle of the floor and blindfold her. The single ladies make a circle around her. The bride spins in one direction and the ladies rotate around her in the opposite direction. When the music stops everyone stops moving and the one the bride is facing is the one to get the bouquet.

This gave us the best of both worlds. Great photos and lively interaction created without any worries for the bride's flowers being ruined. The beauty of doing this is when you follow it with a really lively dance tune which has relevance to the bride and her friends. The music selection may be one from the past when they were all at school or university. It could be something very current which featured on the hen's night. Whatever the music choice it will enable you to go into full party mode within a matter of minutes and move from the formal to the fun and funky part of the evening. Now you can relax and get on with reading your dance floor and playing all of those requests you have been given.

The end is nigh

It is often said that the most important parts of the day from an entertainment point of view are the beginning and the end. What happens in between is important but inevitably the lasting memories are generated in these two time frames. So how should we end a party?

Years ago parties used to fade out with a number of slow romantic tracks being played. These days it is often a livelier ending which is required. In meetings I would often suggest a couple of scenarios. Usually the choice would go like this:

High energy – Low energy – High energy
Or
Low energy – High energy – Low energy

Both variations work but in a different way. Again, what is important is how this is communicated to the guests and how the activity is managed, directed and produced.

An example of a low energy ending could be a slow song to indicate the end of the night is approaching. This is then followed by a high energy item such as Queen's 'Don't stop me now'.

Finally, you may finish on a repeat of the bride and groom's first dance or maybe something which sends a message to all remaining guests. Tunes like 'Perfect day', or 'Thank you' spring to mind.

An example of a high energy finish would go something like this. It may be that you play something like 'Don't stop me now' or 'Dirty dancing' before playing a slow romantic tune. Then to finish you would crank up the volume to play the last tune: "We can't finish tonight without playing our bride and groom's favourite club anthem. This is how they want to end the evening; let's see everyone on the dance floor". You get the picture.

As ever what we are trying to achieve is something personal to the bride and groom. It will be their music selection and it will presented in a manner in which they are comfortable. Your objective is to ensure that the guests stay to the end and that they are included and have a memorable party; send them home wanting more and you will have achieved your goal. Less is best.

It is so much better to finish on a high rather than to allow the proceedings to just fizzle out. You have it in your power to almost predict how an event will evolve from start to finish. The secret is good research, plenty of planning and a sprinkling of inspiration and expertise from you, the professional wedding DJ.

5] EXPLORING YOUR CLIENT'S VISION

Previously I have explained that the main aim of your marketing thus far is to prompt the potential customer to make contact with you. We should not expect them to buy at the first or second point of contact but rather understand that the process will require building relationships based upon trust and respect.

I have suggested that the best way to begin this process is to offer to meet with them in order for you to get a better understanding of what they want from you as an entertainer and also so that you may know more about them.

Where best to meet?

I prefer meeting at their home. Knowing where they live and seeing the type of house or apartment they live in will give you useful information. What kind of area is it? Which type of car do they drive? What are their tastes in furniture and décor? Do they have any children? However, do be careful and do not jump to conclusions based on a limited amount of information. Generally, though, the more you can build up a picture based on what you see and what they tell you, the more you will be able to evaluate whether or not you can do business together.

In their home they are more likely to be relaxed and feel in control. Remember this is not a hard sell. In fact, there should be no hint of 'sales' at this initial meeting. Peter Merry has a very good suggestion which I am happy to recommend you adopt. When meeting with clients for the first time you say nothing about you or your business for the first fifteen minutes other than usual introductions and small talk. Your mission is to allow them to talk about themselves and their vision. You need to know everything about them to allow you to create a proposal which will impress and convince them that you are the DJ for them.

If it is not possible to hold the meeting at their place then the next best place would either be at your office if you have one or maybe at the venue where the reception is being held.

You could also arrange to meet in a nearby hotel lobby or maybe in a local coffee shop if that is convenient. You need to be aware that wherever you hold the meeting there will be distractions and you should try to keep them to a minimum. Remember to turn off your phone and be aware of the time. Keeping the meeting focused and on track will be appreciated.

Two ears and one mouth – use them in that proportion

This meeting is not about you, it's about them. Encourage them to tell you how things are going and where they are up to in the planning process. Do they have any problems with other service providers, maybe you can help? How do they see their big day, what is their vision? Encourage them to take you through the day, step by step from the very beginning. This may seem irrelevant, especially if you have only been invited to discuss the evening entertainment. Bear with me; it will pay dividends later.

People like to talk about themselves and brides love to talk about wedding plans so you should have no problem extracting the information. Your biggest challenge will be to refrain from interrupting every time you hear an opportunity to offer (sell) one of your services. Remember to keep quiet and only interject to prompt for more details. The first fifteen minutes belongs to them.

I would strongly recommend you take notes and ideally have a pre-prepared wedding day work sheet with you so that you can fill in the details as you go. Try to obtain the names of the bridal party. Knowing who the parents are and the names of the best man and chief bridesmaid will help you enormously on the day. Likewise you need to find out which other service providers you may be working with. Photographers, videographers, casino operators, you know the kind of thing.

Encourage them to talk about the venue and who will be supervising – or not, as the case may be – the proceedings. Do they have a Toastmaster? Who are they dealing with on a daily basis at the venue? Will they be there on the day? What about room dressing, have they organised any special decorations you need to be aware of? What is the timeline for the day? Are they getting married in church, at a registry office or at a hotel? How many guests? Will they be with you all day? Are there more guests arriving in the evening and if so how many? What time will they arrive? What time will you have your first dance? Is there food to be served in the evening? The list is endless and the reason you need to know as much as possible is …

"You don't know what you don't know."

The more detail you have the more you can build up a picture of how the bride and groom see their big day unravelling. Their vision is their reality; however, it is also your challenge. The reality is that there may be a problem because surprise surprise …

"They don't know what they don't know."

They have the ideas; YOU have the knowledge and the expertise. You have the ability to turn their vision into reality. Sometimes this will require some tact and diplomacy. Great wedding receptions don't just happen. They need careful planning and more importantly someone in control to ensure that those plans work successfully. As an experienced DJ you are in an ideal situation to bring the whole thing together

Always ask "WHY"?

I love this question. It takes people off guard when you ask it. It's like being a child again. It reminds me of how I feel when a child repeatedly asks "Why" and you find yourself going into ever-increasingly detailed explanations of your reasoning. "Why" is a most powerful question when used in a sales process. The more you know about your client's reasoning the more you will be able to achieve their vision.

This line of questioning is not for the faint-hearted and needs to be handled diplomatically but the results can be eye opening and jaw dropping. Imagine sitting down with a bride and groom and asking, "So why are you getting married?" Let's add a few more 'why' questions.

"Why this year?"
Why not last year or next year, what is significant about this year?

"Why this venue?"
What is so special about this place? What is it that made you decide to have your wedding reception here and not the hotel down the road?

"Why this date?"
Is it a special day, a birthday or an anniversary? Was it the only date available? Were there other factors to be considered, i.e. work commitments, honeymoon, etc.?

"Why a church / registry office / venue wedding?"
There may be strong religious reasons or the complete opposite thinking going on here. It could be a destination wedding, or a fairy-tale wedding in a castle or something similar.

"Why are you getting married at 1.00 p.m.?"
Who determined that time? It could be the venue, the photographer or it may again be down to the registrar or venue.

Is it the 'ideal' time or has a compromise been reached?

"Why bother getting married at all, what was the deciding factor?"
The answer to this can take you in many directions but their reply can be most informative. You may well reveal the 'magic' which underpins the reasoning for the whole celebration.

"Why Gary for your best man?"
Is he related, or maybe an old school friend or perhaps a work colleague or maybe a fellow member of a sports team?

"Why Susan for your chief bridesmaid?"
Same as above, why her and what is her special connection to the bride?

"Why have a first dance?"
Good question. Some bride and grooms will not want one; however, asking them the question will reveal whether they have actually thought about it or are they doing it because it is expected of them?

"Why did you choose that piece of music for your first dance?"
Again, we are looking for the story. Any pieces of information which personalises this music to them will help you when it comes to making that special announcement.

"Why book a DJ for the wedding reception?"
Have they considered the alternatives? What do they expect from you?

"Why are you finishing the reception at 2.00 a.m.?"
Because that is the time the bar closes? Is it a realistic assumption that guests will have had enough long before this time or will the party still be in full swing? How would you achieve this?

When exploring your client's vision you also need to keep relating their vision to your experience. We are talking here about what they perceive will happen at any given moment and what you know could happen. Many such scenarios will be covered later in the section of the book which covers 'staging', which is how we plan, produce and direct interactive parts of the wedding reception.

A key part of their vision and the success of the event will be dependent on how much they commit to the proceedings. The more they are involved the more successful the outcome will be. Alan Marshall, a well-respected DJ / MC from Andover put it like this.

He asks his brides, "Where is the party going to be?"

He explains that the party will take place wherever the bride and groom choose to be. Guests will inevitably focus on them and will want to be in their company whenever possible. So if you have a bride and groom who sit at the bar all night or, worse still, are outside in the smoking area, guess what, that's where the party will be. This has major implications for you as the DJ.

If you can keep a bride in particular on the dance floor for most of the night you will have a good chance of keeping all of her friends and family on the floor as well. This would be ideal but by no means should be relied upon.

However, explaining this relationship between her and her guests will help you when suggesting a few ideas you may have for interaction. Placing the spotlight on a bride and her husband at the right time can be a great way of breaking up the evening and reminding guests that this is not just another party but their wedding reception.

Why bother with this process of interview?

By delving deep into the thought process of why the wedding is taking place you will 'connect' with your client. They will understand that you 'care' about them and the success of their wedding reception. If you can demonstrate that you are striving to be creative and that the outcome will be a fantastic party which their guests will remember for years after the date, why would they consider another DJ or form of entertainment?

It may seem a little daunting at first and also a little invasive. Once you get the right mix of sincerity and curiosity in your interview technique clients will warm to you. Remember people buy people. If they like and trust you and believe that you have their best interests at heart they will work with you to produce a memorable wedding reception.

I have provided a copy of a template which I use to record details at a meeting. This document forms the basis of my work sheet for the event. This provides me with all the names and timings which helps to keep me focused and the event on track.

6] WHY BOOK YOU?

One good reason

A client needs only one good reason to book you. Not two or three reasons: just one is all that's needed. Sometimes we are so keen to reel off all that we do in a never-ending list of 'me, me, me' that we miss this vital point. Sometimes you can talk yourself into, and out of, a booking.

It could be something special or something different, or something bigger or better or something quirky and off the wall. All it takes is one thing. The challenge we have is identifying what that one thing is. Also we need to recognise that this one good reason to be booked will be different depending on the client. We all have different tastes so logically our clients do too.

So our challenge is first of all to have a number of 'services' which are unique to us and for us to be able to relate them to our clients. Once the client has understood what we have to offer we need to capitalise on that one good reason.

Sitting in front of a bride when she is planning her wedding, it is no surprise that most are concerned about the music and dancing. Brides believe that this is the most important issue when booking a DJ; however, after a wedding the priorities are often changed. In most cases after a wedding a bride says she most valued being able to relax and enjoy the party. Peace of mind allowed her to enjoy the moment knowing that her entertainment professional would deliver a great experience.

Peace of mind may well be that one reason to book you. If you can build up a collection of testimonials which support the fact that you care about the success of the event, and have every circumstance covered, brides will have confidence in you.

Fear and emotion

Fear plays a big part in the booking process. If you can overcome a bride's fears then you are halfway to getting her business. Many brides have been to other people's weddings. Some have even been married before. If you ask the simple question, "What did you like about those weddings?", she will tell you the kind of things she would like incorporated into her big day. Even more powerful is the question, "What did you NOT like about the weddings you have attended?"

This often gives you ideas of what not to suggest; however, it may just give you the opportunity to explore her reasoning in more detail. It may be that she didn't like something because of 'the way' it was portrayed. Some things like the garter ceremony can come across as being tacky and in bad taste if done badly. On the other hand, a garter ceremony presented well and in accordance with the taste of your client can be a very enjoyable and memorable part of the evening. It's not what you do; it's the way that you do it!

What is there for a bride to fear?

DJ will not turn up:

It happens; we all get calls on a Saturday night from people whose DJ has failed to show. How do you overcome this fear? Firstly being able to say truthfully that this has never happened with your company will go a long way to allaying this issue. Explaining your 'plan B' is crucial. If you are a multi-operator this situation is usually rectified by having a list of DJs who you can call on at a moment's notice. This is where networking with other DJs and especially within associations will pay dividends. If you are a single operator you have a bigger challenge. Cars can refuse to start or break down en route to the venue. We all get ill from time to time. Accidents happen!

Your plan B needs to be detailed. Ideally you should always have someone at the end of a phone who can help you out of a tight spot. This is easy to say but not at all easy to do. At the higher level I would suggest that you need to have a partner, associate, roadie, etc. who can step in at the last minute if only to provide a basic functional disco experience.

It is a good idea to have a reference to such a situation written into your contract. It may well be that compensation should be payable to the client if you specifically cannot perform due to illness or accident. If such an illness or accident prevails in the days leading up to an event it would be as well to include a provision for you to provide a substitute DJ of similar experience to yourself. I would also allow the client to refuse this offer and to go elsewhere without any penalty.

Sound system breaks down:

You should actually expect this to happen, because it will. One day Murphy's Law will strike you down when you least expect it. The simple answer is to have two of everything with you at all times. I had my van partitioned and divided into two halves.

In the back was my main performance system. In the front was my smaller but equally professional back-up system. I would also always carry my case of compact discs even though I now play music on a computer with MP3 files.

DJ inappropriately dressed:

There really isn't any excuse for this. The dress code should have been agreed at the planning stage. Ask the question, do the research and show the client exactly what you will be wearing on the day. I would suggest going the extra mile. Don't just turn up in jeans and a sweater to set up the equipment. Instead invest in some quality work wear bearing your name or company logo. Look professional at all times. Change into your performance attire when appropriate and take pride in your appearance.

DJ doesn't have the first dance song or plays wrong version:

Yes, this happens, apparently far more frequently than it should. There can be quite a few challenges these days when it comes to specific music requests. A first-dance tune is probably the most important tune of the day. Making sure that you have it is paramount. Making sure that it is the right version is another major challenge in some cases. Many song titles start off as an album track. These are frequently then edited down for a release as a 'single'. Occasionally the track may be rerecorded or remixed especially if it appears in a film or as an advertisement on television. The golden rule here is to check with the client. Take the recording with you and play it to them at a meeting prior to the event.

Sometimes brides offer to bring the song along on the day. Fine; however, I would only accept this as a last resort. Ideally I would offer to collect it or have it posted to me before the event. This gives you the opportunity to confirm that the format is acceptable for your sound system. I have had clients bring me a piece of music on a CD only to find that it is recorded on a DVD in a file format which I could not play! Fortunately I had sourced my own version independently.

I would always recommend that you have the first-dance song available in as many formats as your sound system can accommodate. I would have the song on my laptop in MP3 and WAV format. I would also have it copied to a CD (check licensing law) and even have it stored on my iPhone, just in case.

DJ drunk on the job:

No excuse for this, but guess what, brides have told me they have seen it happen. Unfortunately some DJs seem to think that it is acceptable to drink alcohol at a wedding, especially if there is a free bar. Have it written into your contract. "I will not consume alcohol at your event". Peace of mind for your client and a guarantee from you is all that is required.

DJ uses inappropriate language:

Unfortunately some DJs do not realise that the words they use can be offensive to others. It may well be that certain words and slang terms are becoming more and more common in everyday language; however, caution should be exercised at weddings. Remember there are many different age groups and people from all walks of life, sometimes even visitors from overseas. This also extends to the music which you play. You have a duty to be aware of the lyrics used, especially in some current chart material. Always ask your client how they feel about 'adult' or 'offensive' lyrics. My advice would be to always seek out the 'clean' version.

DJ too cheesy!:

Cheesy is subjective, so I would ask the client to explain exactly what their interpretation of the word is. To some people cheesy is old-school seventies and eighties disco whilst to others it can mean any song which is associated with dance routines or hand movements.
I like cheese, especially after a meal! Cheese can be fun but only if it's the right cheese served in the right manner. Check with your client and draw up the boundaries.

DJ too chatty:

This is probably in relation to a bad experience with another DJ at a previous party. There are still DJs out there who insist on talking in-between every track. "That was, this is", you know the guy who insists on telling everyone that the tune got to number whatever in a year we couldn't care less about. However, we do need to communicate with the guests and using a microphone correctly helps create the atmosphere on the dance floor. Explain what your style is and work with your client to deliver just the right amount of microphone use to music playback ratio.

DJ not chatty enough:

Similar to the previous situation this is a reflection on other DJs' style and the client's vision for her night. If you have audio or video to illustrate what you do and how you do it to overcome this fear so much the better. Elsewhere in this book there is an illustration as to how the use of a microphone will change throughout the night. It should help you and your client arrive at a compromise. However, there is always the exception to the rule and I was once asked to provide a full-on, in-your-face Smashy and Nicey party, which is exactly what I delivered. A great time was had by all.

No one dances:

I can't believe that this should even be considered as a fear, but it is. Over the years more than a few brides have told me that they attended other people's weddings and that no one danced. This is something I find hard to believe, but apparently it is true. It happens! Facetiously I used to enquire was the DJ blind, death and dumb because I can't comprehend how this situation could occur. I can honestly say it has NEVER happened to me. Maybe I've been lucky. I would prefer to believe that my research and my willingness to play my client's and her guests' music preferences together with my own selections have stood me in good stead.

It is also worthwhile to point out here that some clients can accidentally contribute to their own downfall. It may be that in those situations where no one danced the DJ was under orders only to play a list of music provided by the client. It could also have been the case that he was told the order in which to play the music. Both you and I know that that is a recipe for disaster. As is an iPod wedding or a jukebox wedding; education is the key. We have the knowledge and the expertise and it is our obligation to pass on what we know for the benefit of our clients.

No requests played:

Again, this could be under the instruction of the client. However, there needs to be some flexibility and trust. If your client understands that you will not play anything offensive or sensitive and that anything borderline will be discussed with them before playing, then all should be well. I would suggest the client draw up a 'do not play' list which helps identify specifically what is not wanted, but this list will also give you an idea as to your client's thinking on the issue.

However, there is another reason why no requests are played and this time the responsibility lies with the DJ. He may not have the music.

His collection does not cover a wide enough range of styles and genres. Sometimes DJs specialise in one genre to the detriment of all others. Worse still, some DJs are of the opinion that they know what is best to play and therefore do not play requests.

Honesty is the best policy. If someone asks for a piece of music I would always play it if I could, but it would be played when I deemed it appropriate. If I did not have the track I would say so and offer to play something similar. Personally I always opted for the policy of "Your night, your music".

Music too loud:

This, I am ashamed to admit, crops up time and time again. Why is it that some DJs have to bring the whole nightclub experience including knee-breaking and ear-splitting volume levels to every event? Great professional gear is fine but it needs to be controlled and used correctly. That's what your mixer and the volume control is for. We need to appreciate that a wedding is not like other parties, at least, not until later on in the evening. Excessive volume can destroy a wedding reception. It can fragment the audience and chase people into the bar, or another room or, worse still, encourage them to leave the celebrations early.

While we are on this subject we should try to separate a couple of areas of confusion. Sometimes excessive volume is confused with distortion. The audio signal can become distorted simply because the mixer, amplifier and speakers are out of balance. It is possible for a relatively low volume level to be distorted which creates a similar, unpleasant output which guests will not appreciate.

Something else I have noticed on this subject. It's always amazed me that you will be asked to turn down the volume usually by someone who doesn't like what you are playing and conversely the same person will tell you to turn up the volume when you play something he or she likes.

Guests are embarrassed by the DJ:

This happens usually because of the style and presentation of the DJ. It's also something which comedians suffer from. You either like them or you don't. It is all down to what the client is comfortable with.

I would always stress that I would never do anything to embarrass a guest at a wedding. However, in order to achieve this I would need to get a good briefing from my client beforehand as to what the guidelines were and which subjects were sensitive. Again, consultation, communication and professionalism all come into play here. If in doubt, leave it out is good advice.

Guests stay in the bar:

This can be a big worry, especially if the bar is in a different room to which the DJ is situated. There are a number of reasons this can happen, some obvious and some less so. A free bar provided by the host can often encourage this behaviour especially if the bar is only free up until a certain time. It can also be an issue if the principal guests, i.e. the bride and groom, insist in taking up station there and buying their guests drinks.

Sometimes it is a man thing. The guys like to stand together and get smashed while the girls are happy to do their own thing. Hopefully in this situation you can encourage the girls to dance; however, depending on the demographic of the guests there may not be enough of them to keep the dance floor busy. At the end of the day all you can do is your best. Work those you have in front of you and be as open and responsive as you can be.

Ironically this is not a hopeless situation. I have had many a 'slow' or 'quiet' night from a dance floor perspective only to be praised at the end for providing "a great night, brilliant music, we really enjoyed it". As the saying goes, nothing is quite so strange as folk.

Buffet is not eaten:

Buffets are not cheap and therefore it is a shame to waste money on food which nobody eats. Whilst it is true to say that this is not a primary responsibility of the DJ it is an area with which he can help. Buffets remain uneaten for a number of reasons. The timing of a buffet is often a contributing factor. The more flexible the caterers are the better chance people will have to eat it. Sometimes there is simply too much food and people are not hungry especially they have been well fed earlier in the day.

From our point of view as DJs I would say we have certain responsibilities. We need to ensure that we announce the food when it is made available. Ideally try to get the bride and groom to 'open' the buffet.

If we encourage others to join the bride and groom at the buffet table then people will not be afraid to be the first to eat.

It also helps if the DJ prompts the guests at regular intervals whilst the food is available and also that he communicates when it will be taken away if that is the case.

A sort of 'last orders' for the food will often result in a last dash from some of the guests. I have known some brides want the DJ not to stop the dance music or change the tempo of music when a buffet is ready to be served. They have a vision of the party not being interrupted and the dancing continuing. This may be a challenge but can be achieved; however, in such circumstances this works better when a 'light supper' is served rather than a full buffet. All we can do as DJs is to share our experiences and make suggestions. Once we know what is expected all we can do is run with it and manage the situation to the best of our ability.

Guests leave early:

This is a nightmare situation which everyone wants to avoid. Hopefully by following some of the advice in this chapter and avoiding the pitfalls this will not happen. Occasionally there are hidden agendas and situations beyond your control. All we can try to do is cover all the bases.

The weather can be a major factor which will cause guests to leave early. Excessive heat can leave people exhausted. We all look forward to a perfect summer's day but sometimes it can work against us, especially when it get up to 38 degrees Celsius.

Rain, snow and ice can have a similar affect. If people are concerned about getting home safely or if transport will not be available they will make an early exit.

Sporting events which clash with the date of the wedding can also have a negative impact on evening receptions. Even though TV programmes can be recorded very few people like the idea of missing out on a live event. It may be that this is actually expected.

Many brides have said to me that the "'oldies' will all be in bed by 11 o'clock so there may only be about forty of us left by then". Fine, we can work with that. Or it may be that a significant number of guests arrived together by coach and that they will be departing at a certain time.

Therefore it makes sense to know who they are and what time they are due to leave. It may be that you create a 'false ending' so that as many people as possible are included in the 'big finish'.

Then you can change tack, call it an after party and work with however many guests are left until the allotted time for you to finish up.

If the idea of people leaving early is a major worry it may be prudent to suggest bringing forward the expected finish time. It may be that it is the venue who has indicated that the party finishes at one o'clock in the morning. Sometimes less is more, especially if people have been up early and on the go all day.

Suggesting a finish at 11.30 when most people will still be there is much better than trying to eke out another hour while your audience deserts you. It has to be so much better to finish on a high and send them home wanting more than to fade away with a whimper.

7] MICROPHONE TECHNIQUE

The first time you stand in front of the guests, open the microphone and speak is your chance to show them that you are NOT a $500 DJ, but a true professional that knows what he's doing. If your announcement is clear, relative, understood and you have everyone's attention, they will all listen to you the next time you speak.

I don't wish to teach grandmothers to suck eggs. What follows is intended to focus your attention on an area of your performance which is of paramount importance if you are to be successful as a specialist wedding DJ/MC.

Over the years we have seen a new breed of DJ who seldom uses a microphone. Instead they prefer to let the music do the talking whilst the dance floor fills. However, I would suggest that whilst this may be acceptable later in the evening, microphone usage is vital to the success of a wedding reception, especially in the first hour or two of an evening party.

The microphone is a tool which needs to be fine-tuned. It is the first piece of equipment in the amplification process and it can help you sound great or it can let you down badly.

Buy the best microphone you can afford. Generally the more you pay the better they are. Seek advice from your local dealer and find one which suits your vocal range. We all sound different and microphones have different characteristics which can help you sound clearer. Some microphones have a warm tone whilst others can make you sound quite sharp or thin. Your voice together with the right microphone will be a major factor in delivering announcements and directions which can be heard and more importantly UNDERSTOOD by everyone in the room.

The microphone should be positioned beneath your mouth and not in front of it. A quality microphone will be sensitive enough to pick up your voice at a range of two to six inches from your mouth. Placing the microphone just below your chin will also enable people to see your full face and will hopefully allow your mouth to form the words as against mumbling into the protective mesh which covers the cartridge. Poor microphone handling can create noise which detracts from what you are saying. Try not to place your hand near the top of the microphone. The best place is usually around the centre of its length or just below the head of the microphone. Better quality microphones are insulated and therefore produce less handling noise.

Try to avoid placing the microphone on hard surfaces or using the on-off switch while leaving the channel open on your mixer. It is much better to close the fader and then switch off the microphone in order to avoid unnecessary click and pops. Some mixers have mute buttons which work even better by allowing you to leave your volume levels constantly set while opening and closing the microphone silently.

Consider using a microphone stand. Placing the microphone on a stand can be a good idea. It will enable you to keep both hands free. This will allow you to hold your script or cue cards whilst adjusting output levels or selecting music to be played. Make sure you position it correctly. Avoid stooping or dropping your head when reading. Talk over the microphone and not into it and you will be fine.

Guests using your microphone

I am never comfortable allowing other people to use my microphone but it is a necessary evil which cannot be avoided. Guests will often need a microphone when making speeches. Grooms will often want to thank their guests for coming at the evening reception and inevitably someone at some time will want to sing a song even if you don't do karaoke!

There are a number of issues to be considered here. Most people have no idea as to how to use a microphone. Women, generally speaking, pardon the pun, have quite 'thin' voices which tend to be high-pitched and difficult to amplify when compared to a man's deeper and lower vocal rage. Men, especially young and excitable men, tend to roar, shout and scream into a microphone which can have disastrous results for your sound system.

I would suggest, if possible, that a guest speaker be coached in the use of the microphone if you have the opportunity. Hopefully this would help avoid the embarrassing situation where they hold the microphone at waist level and point it away from their mouth toward the audience rendering the thing entirely useless.

The same thing can happen with miniature microphones worn on a tie tack or coat lapel. The general public are used to seeing people on TV using microphones in this way and wonder why they cannot be heard on your system. They are blissfully unaware of the fact that in the studio there will be a microphone over the speaker's head and a directional microphone on the floor pointing toward them. We have no such options and have to rely on the single microphone.

Another issue to be considered is that the person may not have heard their voice amplified before. Their natural reaction is to automatically speak softer because they believe they are talking too loudly. The more you increase their volume the softer they tend to speak! A quick practice session or rehearsal will overcome these issues but sometimes you just have to wing it or play it by ear. (More puns, sorry.)

Radio microphone or cable microphone

Ideally both would be my advice. Wired, or cable microphones generally are better quality when compared by cost dollar for dollar. In other words if you are on a tight budget go for a wired microphone. Wired microphones are easier to set up and are less complicated which usually means more reliable if you look after them. The only down side to wired microphones is the length of cable. I would suggest you carry a variety of cable leads of different lengths so that you can cover all situations. Longer cables require more care when in use especially from a health and safety point of view. The last thing you want is someone tripping over the lead.

Radio microphones give you freedom. Freedom to go anywhere in the room and be involved in the action while still able to give a commentary or make announcements without having to worry about, or be restricted by, the cable. Good quality radio microphones are not cheap but they are a great investment. I love my Shure radio microphone and wouldn't be without it. Downside is that you have to do everything else single handed.

If you use a radio microphone please, please, please, insert a new battery or charge the cell before every use. There is nothing worse than a battery going down whilst you or, worse still, a guest is midway through a speech.

Most radio microphones these days operate on a choice of frequencies and the better ones allow you to select from a range built into the transmitter and receiver. You must check out the selection at every venue before you begin your performance. It is possible your frequency will conflict with other systems in the area especially if you are sharing the event with other entertainers. Be professional and be prepared for all such eventualities.

Being confident on the microphone is something which helps set the tone or style of a party. If you come across as warm, friendly and helpful people are more likely to listen to you and do as you ask. Achieving the right mix of authority whilst not wishing to be seen as bossy or arrogant is not easy.

It takes practice and training but in time once you have found the right technique it will pay dividends.

Don't forget to do a sound check before every performance. You need to be certain that you can be heard from anywhere in the room both early on, when music levels are low, and later when your volume is cranked up. Some mixers have a voice over-ride facility which automatically fades the music level when you speak. These can be very useful. There is nothing worse than a DJ shouting over the music.

If all else fails pull down the fader, make your announcement, and return the fader to its original position. Basic stuff it may be but you would be surprised the way some of our colleagues use microphones.

The ten percent rule

It is also wise to understand that people only take notice of ten percent of what is said. If you ramble on and on people will lose interest. Ask yourself, is what you are about to say relevant? Does it add anything of value to the proceedings? Is it necessary? Is it about me or you? Generally speaking, if what you have to say is of no value then don't say it.

When it comes to announcements, less is more. Be aware of redundant phrases. Be short and to the point wherever possible. Let's look at an example of an introduction for a first dance.

A] Ladies and gentlemen, at this time I would like to introduce the bride and groom onto the dance floor for their first official dance as husband and wife. Will you all please be upstanding and give a huge round of applause for Jennifer and Alan, the new Mr and Mrs Jones. (51 words)

B] Ladies and gentlemen, it's time for you to welcome Alan and Jennifer onto the dance floor for their first official dance. I give you the new Mr and Mrs Jones. (30 words)

It is also easier to reduce the number of words if you use music and lighting to support your announcement. In option B] above I would have started with a rousing fanfare to get attention. And have some high energy music like 'Are you ready for this' as my audio bed to generate a dynamic level of energy to accompany my introduction. Therefore I don't need to use as many words in order to achieve the same goal. I would also have switched the colour of my up-lighting when I played the fanfare.

This would send a visual and audio signal to the guests that something significant was about to happen.

In example A], "Will you all please be upstanding and give a huge round of applause ...", the obvious is being stated. If the introduction is made with enthusiasm the guests will naturally stand and applaud.

In the example above we have started to integrate the elements of combined lighting and dynamic music together with more succinct use of the microphone. We are now entering the realms of production. Remember, it's not what you do; it's the way that you do it which makes you stand out from the crowd.

Production and direction can best be described as staging. Staging is a vital part of what we do as successful wedding DJs. The staging makes the difference. Staging creates impact. Impact helps us be remembered for all the right reasons.

Just before we leave the topic of microphone technique it would be as well to remember another aspect. Generally speaking, I would suggest that you use the microphone more in the early part of the evening and less as the night progresses. Usually you will have a lot of information to impart at the beginning including introducing yourself, explaining what is going to happen throughout the night, details of the first dance, etc.

However, as the evening unwinds and the dance floor fills you will find that you only need to speak occasionally. You may need to do a request or transition into a different music genre, or as my friend Mark Walsh would say, "Stir the pot" in order to add energy into the crowd.

8] OPPORTUNITIES RELATED TO WEDDINGS

At first sight, it may appear that a DJ is only required for the evening section of a wedding reception. Many future brides will have no knowledge of the other services which are available. These services are often provided by other service providers and yet there is no reason why these should not be provided by the DJ. Here are some examples:

Equipment hire

Not all venues have their own public address or background music system. Those that do have some kind of system are often not suitable for the purpose. It may well be that the staff do not know how to work the equipment or that the system is poorly maintained and not reliable.

How much better would it be to have a temporary sound system delivered, set up and controlled by a professional, i.e. you? In most cases it would only have been sitting in your storage area or packed in the van waiting for your use later in the day. It may surprise you to learn that a basic sound system comprising of a couple of speakers on stands, a mixer and radio microphone can often cost in excess of $250 to 'dry hire'.

Now we are not talking about anything other than equipment here. This is the kind of equipment rented for 'speeches' at a wedding. The gear would need to be delivered and tested in the morning and collected or repositioned later in the day. If you were the DJ for the evening reception so much the better; half of your sound system is on site and ready to go.

Data projectors

Prices may well have come down over the years and many hotels do have them for hire but at a cost. Do your research and check out if there is an opportunity here for you. I had a couple of hotels close to my base who were always calling to ask if I had one available, often at the last minute. Usually this was because their wedding coordinator had forgotten to include it in her briefing notes or that their own projector was 'missing' or faulty.

Either way the opportunity provided me with extra income to the tune of $100 each time they needed a projector 'dropped off'. Ironically the 'specialist sound and lighting companies' will not be interested in this kind of opportunity. To them this is 'small change'.

Anything under a few hundred dollars is below their radar and besides, most are closed on a Saturday and Sunday.

Mood lighting or up-lighting

This has, in the past few years, provided a great opportunity for DJs to earn extra cash. In the past providing this sort of service involved using high power light units with plastic gels to create the desired colour. This required access to dedicated power supplies and also raised issues of heat generated by the lamps which had implications for health and safety. This all changed with the introduction of light emitting diode (LED) technology. These new LED up-lighters not only drew about a tenth of the power of previous units but they were also able to change colour instantly, thanks to built-in DMX circuitry. Once again the costs tumbled and the specialist hire companies left a gap in the market for those DJs with the knowledge and motivation to move in on this market. For the first time the idea of providing up-lighting at a wedding reception in a local venue became cost effective and within budget for many more brides.

A room could be transformed instantly from a cool corporate cream into a warm pink or violet colour at the touch of a button. Later in the evening it would also be possible to have the whole room bouncing with light as the system changed colour to the beat of the music. One system could create a stylish, sophisticated atmosphere or a funky disco kaleidoscope for very little money. I would suggest that this service could be offered for anything between $300 and $600 with ease. I also found that the best way to market the up-lighting packages was to offer to light a function room the next time the venue was having an 'open day' or evening show round. Even the hotel staff were amazed at the difference in their room once the lighting had been set up and switched on. I loved it when a potential client would express an interest in the lighting. In order to prove just how much it enhanced the room I would simply turn it off! Seeing the room in its normal everyday light would be enough to convince the bride that she had to have my up-lights.

Music for a civil ceremony

We have mentioned this elsewhere in the book. In this section I will explain the logistics and the value which relates to this opportunity. It has to be said that most venues have no idea what it takes to theme a civil wedding when it comes to music. At best they will have a couple of CDs probably containing the traditional music taken from church weddings in the past. Or they will simply rely on the bride and groom to create their own disc which

73

the venue will offer to play. Neither of which is satisfactory or worthy of such an important event as a wedding ceremony. Especially as this music is often delivered to the audience's ears by an inferior public address system.

The mobile DJ has the knowledge and the equipment together with the skill to not only offer advice on music selection but also to play that music so that it has the desired effect. Music levels change throughout a recording, especially classical and instrumental tracks. Here you have an opportunity to get under the skin of the bride and groom and put together a selection of music which reflects their personalities and which creates the atmosphere which they desire. You have the equipment to present that music in the way it was originally intended: dynamically, powerfully and emotionally.

Remember, your sound system should be discreet. Ideally your equipment rack or work station should take up less than one square metre of floor space. Make sure all your cables and wires are hidden and on no account display any form of advertising. This is not about you. Pricing for this service is open for interpretation. I would say that it could be included as part of a package or as a standalone option.

Master of Ceremonies

This is something which I refer to throughout this book and it is a very lucrative opportunity for those who wish to assume these duties. However, a word of warning is needed. This is not something to be undertaken lightly. I would direct your attention the first word, 'Master'. Unless you appreciate and understand the role of an MC then do not attempt to be one.

Toastmasters have to undergo formal training in all aspects of function etiquette and the art of formal speaking as well as making introductions before they can pull on the famous red coat and wear the gold medallion. Many venues will have a recommended Toastmaster or will offer their own member of staff as a MC.

There is another option which is you, the DJ, as the MC.

I would suggest that you approach this as a third choice and middle option. Positioning yourself under the Toastmaster but above the hotel employee should illustrate how you see yourself and give an indication as to your worth to the client. Toastmasters generally, but not always, tend to foster the image of being like a sergeant major. They come across as being formal and strict, often bossy.

This is understandable, particularly as they have a responsibility to maintain a timeline and that their background is often one of a military nature.

Some brides and grooms may like the idea of having someone to take on this responsibility and make the announcements but would prefer such duties to be discharged in a more relaxed manner. This is where I see the DJ as an ideal alternative. You can be the friend of the family who is detached from the wedding party but able to comprehend their wishes and with the ability to represent them in a manner with which they are comfortable.

Check out how much Toastmasters earn in your area. I would suggest many charge anything between $400 and $1000 on average for three to four hours work. There has to be an opportunity here for the mobile DJ, especially when you consider some of the alternatives provided by venue staff.

I should also like to mention here that there are places you may wish to go in order to seek formal training so that you may be better placed to undertake these duties and responsibilities. Toastmasters International has a training programme which all DJs can benefit from. They specialise in training people to speak in public. There are also individual professional speakers who offer such services.

I would personally recommend the training I received from Mark and Rebecca Ferrell. Their 'MarBecca Method' training is excellent. Contact details can be found at the rear of this book.

Dance Floors

Brides are always on the lookout for the next 'wow' factor. Decorating the tables and chairs as well as lighting the walls is all very nice but what about the floor? Many venues have a traditional wooden dance floor which is either a permanent fixture or they use a portable product which is laid at the appropriate time. However, there is a better alternative. Portable dance floors are now being produced from new materials.

Companies are able to supply black and white, chequered dance floors. They are also able to incorporate LED technology or fibre optics to produce a dance floor which changes colour or sparkles and glitters. These new dance floors are providing that extra 'wow' factor which your clients may well be seeking. These dance floors can be expensive to produce and acquire which means that rental rates are very profitable for those who choose to invest in them.

Additional opportunities

So far I have concentrated on opportunities related to our vocal skills or our knowledge and access to sound and lighting. There are other opportunities for you to sell products and services to your bride and groom; however, I would advise caution here. If these products or services do not interfere with your commitments and responsibilities as a DJ / MC then all is well. If, however, offering additional items will distract you and need your attention then I would urge you not to do anything other than DJ/MC. It may be that the following suggestions can be offered by colleagues and be totally independent from you on the day in which case by all means look to add these enhancements to your services.

Video recording:

This can be a great service to offer. It will not only record all of the memorable events of the occasion but it will by its very nature be something which features you and your DJ/MC talent. You will have control of the editing process and will have collaborated with your client in order to produce a story board which will show off your hosting and entertainment skills. Use of such footage could be used to showcase what you do to prospective clients. Obviously you would need permission to share such footage in this way.

Still photography:

These days just about everyone has a camera and thanks to digital imaging the cost of processing is cheaper than it's ever been. However, great photography is not about the tools; it's about the creative genius behind the lens. So unless you are qualified I would stay out of this market.

Some DJs have, however, found a niche market offering novelty mementos at the evening reception providing key rings or place mats with images taken informally at the party. These can be quite popular and profitable if done correctly. A variation on this theme is the 'photo booth'.

The photo booth:

This could possibly have been included in the first section depending on the level of sophistication of the booth. The idea is that you provide a booth similar to those which we have traditionally used to obtain passport photos. These booths come in a variety of shapes and sizes together with price tags to match.

I have seen about half a dozen examples at trade shows and they are indeed becoming more popular at wedding receptions. Some require the use of an operator while others are coin operated and could in theory be left unattended.

In principle the idea is that informal, spontaneous photographs of one or more guests can be produced in a few moments. The print being available in a few minutes! Some systems automatically produce a second copy which is kept for the client so that they have a photographic record of who had their pictures taken on the night. Sometimes these are offered in a folder or book format.

The chocolate fountain:

These have been popular for many years now and are still popular; however, health and safety legislation and hygiene regulations can be an issue. Love them or hate them, many DJs have bought them and earned good money from them.

Candy tables:

The idea of providing a table or cart full of the kind of candy or sweets which we used to buy as kids is very novel. Children at a wedding reception will love them and when you think about it we were all kids once so even the adults like this too. Highly profitable to the DJ and the benefit to the client is that they get to keep all of the sweets even if they are not all eaten on the day.

Proceed with caution:

The list of other products and services available is really quite extensive. I will provide more suggestions below. Please take care: while you may be looking to help your client obtain extra value and have the convenience of only dealing with one company the responsibility increases with each extra service you provide. You may purchase these items and manage the whole process using your own staff; however, it is more customary to sub-contract these services to other providers.

Sub-contracting can be risky. If you rely on others to provide these services you will no longer be in control. Quality may suffer and you will be held accountable should the service not live up to expectations or, worse still, fail to be delivered.

Other products which may be offered to your clients:

Interactive games consoles can be a great way to keep children entertained, especially during times when they would naturally be bored. The idea of having a play area in another room where children can be entertained using latest technology is a really good one. Systems like the 'Nintendo Wii' can also be used for adult amusement later in the day.

Casino Tables:

Great for corporate entertainment but not something I would recommend for a wedding. I have worked at a number of weddings where they have been present and I understand why a bride may wish to have them; however, it is my opinion that they distract from the music and fragment the guests. In other words there is too much going on. If a client wanted to have a casino theme then I would work closely with them to ensure that nothing clashed with my performance or any other planned activity. Sometimes it can be a case of trying to put too much into a small amount of time.

Fireworks display:

These should only be undertaken by qualified licence holders in accordance with local authority permission. Timing of these displays needs to be coordinated taking into account weather conditions, sunset time and catering requirements.

Chinese lanterns:

There can be some health and safety issues with the flying of Chinese lanterns, especially if you are located under a commercial flight path. It is advisable to check with the venue to ensure that they are happy with this activity. Some will not be happy and may refuse permission based on complaints from local residents who are left with the remaining debris after the lanterns have fallen back to the ground.

Public liability policy:

Finally, please check your public liability insurance before offering or taking part in any activities outside of your core business of playing music. If in doubt seek advice from your insurer or your professional DJ association (djaa.com.au in Australia).

9] WHAT'S YOUR USP?

Unique selling point

Every successful business has a USP so logically every successful disc jockey should also have a unique selling point. What is it about you that is unique? It could be argued that by our very nature we are all different. We come in all shapes and sizes. We have differing skin colours and talk with many accents. Our personalities can be very different and our behaviour or attitude can alter depending upon the circumstances we find ourselves in. So how do you define yourself to others? Besides your music selection and programming skills, why should a bride book you?

Personality

The thread running through this book is "it's not what you do; it's the way that you do it that gets results". So we also need to understand what it is that you bring to the party which no other DJ does in your market. Perhaps it's your style of presentation. Some DJs can be very loud and proud and in your face while others are very understated and conservative when they perform. Which are you? More importantly, how do you communicate your style to potential clients? When we look at other DJs' websites we tend to see a great many video clips of people dancing but not so many of a DJ making announcements or introductions. Perhaps there should be clips of you showing your versatility by making the same introductions in different styles?

Appearance

These days it well may be that it is your appearance and that of your equipment which makes you stand out from the competition. More and more brides and event planners are concentrating on the 'look' of the event. They are looking for a more minimalist image and no longer want DJs with large rigs and wires trailing all over the place. Knowing how you will be dressed on the day of the event is important to your client. If you are willing to dress in a way which complements the event then you are already ahead of the game. The introduction of more compact but still powerful speaker systems, and cloth-covered DJ booths, has enabled DJs to comply with this new look and even, in some cases, charge a premium for what they supply.

LED and fibre optic lighting has also helped DJs create new and interesting light shows, often incorporating new lightweight lasers which are far less 'in your face' than they used to be. Generally the new adage is 'less is more'.

Guarantee

Do you offer a guarantee? If not, why not? If you are confident that you will deliver all that you promise to a client why shouldn't you offer a guarantee? A guarantee will underpin all of your marketing and prove that you will deliver everything in your contract. I'm not necessarily talking about a 'money back' guarantee here, although there is no reason why one should not be offered. Your guarantee could be based upon what you bring to the event or the time you arrive and are ready to start playing music. It could be that you 'guarantee' not to let the client down and that no matter what should happen a DJ will be provided at the venue on the due date. It takes guts and great confidence to offer a money back guarantee but I do know DJs who do just that. They are so confident that their clients will receive great value for money that if they are not totally satisfied then they can have their money back. Scary but true; however, what a great unique selling point to offer your clients.

Custom recordings and sound drops

It may not always be possible for a family member or special friend to attend the wedding. Years ago telegrams were sent by those who could not attend and their telegrams were read aloud by the best man. Nowadays, thanks to cheap telecommunications and the internet, it is possible to record messages from around the world with ease. Imagine the bride and groom hearing, or seeing, an absent guest thanks to you having the ability to make the recording and then play it back on your audio / video system. Seemingly little things like this can make a big impact on the day's celebrations.

Imagine being able to record the bride and groom's wedding vows from earlier in the day and then editing them so you could use them as sound drops later in the evening. Many of the evening guests will not have been present at the ceremony. How thrilled would they be to hear those vows, do you think? It may be that you simply play them during the buffet or better still how about during their first dance? A lot would depend on the choice of music and the cooperation of your bride and groom but the outcome would be a truly memorable and unique moment. You could even present the recording to them as a memento of their wedding.

A similar opportunity exists for those brides who elect to have a father and daughter dance. You could arrange to record a couple of sound bites from the father which relate to how he is feeling and his best wishes for his daughter and new husband. You would probably need to do this in the days leading up to the wedding. Imagine the surprise on the faces of not only the bride but the entire audience when they hear the father's voice dropped into the lyrics of their song? This is not something to be undertaken lightly but once again, done well, it can be a show stopper and a highly emotional moment.

Interaction

In many instances a great wedding reception requires more than just great music. We often hear from other DJs who report that their recent booking never really got off the ground. We hear that very few people danced and that the crowd "was not up for a party". It happens! If we only rely on music and the audience is not responding, what are we to do? How can we save the party? What can we do to entertain the guests so that we can revisit the dance floor later when their appetite for dancing may have returned?

Snowball dance

Years ago at what we would describe as 'tea dancers' there was a piece of interaction called a 'snowball dance'. The idea was simple. The band leader would ask a couple to go and get two more couples out of the audience to join them on the dance floor. After a short while he would stop the music and invite all of those on the dance floor to do the same. Before long the dance floor was full of dancers. You could do the same with the bride and groom at a wedding.

Longest married dance

You could ask for all of the married couples in the room to join the bride and groom on the dance floor. Ideally both sets of parents will already be on the floor and you should encourage them to identify and invite their married guests to get onto the dance floor. This idea requires the DJ to play a suitable piece of music, preferably slow and romantic which guests of all ages will be happy to dance to. During the dance the music will be stopped and those couples who have been married less than two years should be invited to sit down. After a short while those who have been married less than five years should be invited to sit down. This process is repeated until you find the couple on the dance floor who have been married the longest.

It's a nice touch to reward them and congratulate them maybe with a bottle of wine or flowers.

This idea can also be staged in reverse; you ask all the married couples to stand and invite them to join the bride and groom on the dance floor for a dance, and give the newlyweds some advice on a happy marriage, starting with those most recently married. Eventually you will end up with a full dance floor and the longest married couple still standing where you could find out their names and how many years they have been married and over the microphone ask them to reveal the secret to their long marriage.

Bouquet toss

This is a good way to kick-start a dance floor. Sometimes with the knowledge and approval from the bride and groom, I use this straight after a break for a meal but it can be used anytime. Invite all the single ladies onto the floor. For the purpose of this interaction I would suggest that we ignore the single status and invite as many women as we can get onto the dance floor. The more the better. Position your bride at one end of the floor and have all the other women line up along the opposite side. Play something suitable like 'Girls just wanna have fun'.

Invite any men who may have cameras to come and join you and make sure they get the best shots. Ideally have the bride do a false throw so that the photographer can get a good shot of the bouquet about to leave the bride's hands. Repeat the exercise; substitute your artificial bouquet if the bride does not wish to throw her own. This time have the photographers focus on the line of catching girls. Count down the action and watch the girls scramble to catch the bouquet. Encourage a big cheer and round of applause for the girl who caught it and then play a lively, 'girly' tune to keep all of the women on the floor. In folk law the girl who catches the bouquet is deemed likely to be the next married. Congratulations!

The garter ceremony

Proceed with caution, this is not for the faint-hearted; however, if you have a young bride and groom who are up for a party then this can be very entertaining. The basic idea is that the bride is wearing a garter underneath her dress and that the groom is invited to remove it in front of the assembled guests. Place a chair in the centre of the floor and have the bride sit down. Position the groom in front of her and have him kneel down. Explain what he has to do and then make the task more difficult by telling the groom he can't use his hands.

Earlier you will have explained to the bride that she can assist her husband by raising her dress just enough to reveal the garter and protect her modesty.

She should also extend her leg forward a little so that the groom can reach the garter without too much trouble. Once again some suitable music should be played to add dynamics to what is happening on the floor. You may wish to ask the bride and groom for their music preference. This is also another great way for the groom to put his personality and spin on it. I simply ask what the groom does for a living or his hobbies and try to incorporate that somehow; for example, he might be a motor mechanic and he gets on his creeper and slides under the dress with spanner in hand.

Toss the garter

Once the garter has been retrieved the groom may wish to toss the garter to a group of assembled single men. This is basically the exact same routine as in the bouquet toss with the roles reversed. Again, a suitable macho tune should be played while the men wait to catch the garter as it flies through the air. There are many suggestions of alternate ways to remove or toss the garter. The most important thing to remember is to HAVE FUN.

1) Can toss both garter and bouquet at the same time
2) Can place a $10 or $20 bill in the garter to 'sweeten the pot'
3) Place the garter around a football or basketball then toss it

Next married

Finally the guy who caught the garter should be invited to place it on the leg of the girl who caught the bouquet. The folk law here is that they will be the next couple to be married. This is where you need to take your lead from the bride and groom who are likely to know the two people concerned and who will have an idea as to whether the girl is comfortable with what is about to happen. If she is OK with this then fine, proceed. If she is not then simply encourage her to extend her arm so that the garter may be placed there and not on her leg. Have a lively piece of music ready for the men and women to dance to: 'Girls and boys' by Blur usually goes down well.

Dance off

Pitching the boys against the girls is always a sure-fire method of injecting energy into a dance floor. There are various different ways of achieving this, all of which work well. Usually it involves the girls dancing to a mega girly hit while the boys dance to a typically huge macho piece of music. It can be interesting to reverse the roles and watch what happens. Guys and girls can either dance individually or en masse, the choice is yours.

Do whatever you believe will get the most impact! The dance off is fun to take part in and also for seated guests to enjoy. All you need to do is keep a running commentary and encourage those taking part, as well as deciding who the winners are! Imagine how much fun it could be if you blindfolded the participants; not only fun for them but I bet almost everyone in the room, even the venue staff, will get a laugh out of it.

The shoe game

This is a version of the 'Mr and Mrs' game. The idea is to find out how well our new bride and groom actually know each other. The DJ will ask a series of questions and both the bride and groom will answer simultaneously by holding up either a lady's shoe or a man's shoe. Position the bride and groom on chairs which have been placed on the dance floor back to back. Get them to take off their shoes and swap one of each with each other. They should now both be holding his and her shoes.

Again, another opportunity for the bride and groom to inject their personalities and make it unique; instead of using their shoes they might use Disney soft toys because they both love Disney movies.

Explain that you will ask a question and that they need to answer the question by holding up the shoe which best fits the answer. There are a number of examples and variations on this game to be found on YouTube. Take a look and then adapt what you see to suit your clients. The humour and fun come from the hesitation and agreement or disagreement revealed by their answers. Here is a comprehensive list of questions for you to use.

"Out of the two of you …"
-who made the first move?
-who's the better cook?
-who said "I LOVE YOU" first?
-who has the wackiest family?
-who's the better driver?
-who's the faster driver?
-who spends the most time in front of a mirror?
-who is in control of the check book?
-who wears the pants in the family?

-who is in charge of the remote?
-who spends the most time getting ready to go out?
-who will be doing most of the yard work?
-if you haven't already ... who is most likely to pass gas in front of the other first?
-now that you're married, who will be the first to say ... "Not tonight"?
-who's the better kisser?
-who will be the first to fall asleep tonight?
-who has the smelliest feet?
-who steals the covers more?
-who popped the question?
-who says "I love you" the most in one day?
-who talks more?
-who's most likely to use up all the hot water?
-who's most likely to get lost?
-who's most likely to ask for directions?
-who's the first one to make up after a fight?
-who's the one that started the fight in the first place?
-who's the most likely to wake up grumpy in the morning?
-who's most likely to wake up with a hangover in the morning?
-who's most likely to be running late?
-who spends more money?

Usually you are encouraged to ask this question last in order to finish on a romantic note.

"Who do you love the most in the whole wide world?"

Thank the bride and groom for being great sports and the audience for their attention and support.

Living guest book

This is something which was shared with me by a Canadian DJ at my first visit to Mobile Beat in Las Vegas. The idea is simple and combines the beast of pre-prepared interaction with the spontaneity which can only come from a live interactive experience.

I would begin by explaining that a traditional guest book is often to be found at a wedding reception. It is there for guests to record their sentiments and best wishes for the bride and groom. Often the first couple of pages are filled with interesting, humorous and romantic messages but all too often these are reduced to simple, one-line "Best wishes" or "What a great day", etc. There must be a better way so the living guest book was created.

I suggest using this while guests are enjoying the dinner/buffet. I will use the buffet for my example. Once the food has been served and the guests are seated I would explain that we are about to do something different which they have never seen before. I would explain that everyone in the room is here because they know the happy couple and wouldn't it be nice if they could all give them one piece of advice which would help them in their married life. This may be advice which was shared with you when you got married or it may be something which you learnt yourself, the hard way, when living together. Either way, this advice can be practical, romantic, funny or downright rude. It's up to you! To help you there are four prompt cards which begin:

To have a long and happy married life I would …
To have a long and happy married life the one thing never to do is …
To have a long and happy married life the one thing never to say is …
To have a long and happy married life the one thing I'd like to tell the opposite sex is …

All you have to do is complete the sentence. Also, please be aware that you need to complete the bottom of the card by telling us who you are and what your relationship is to the bride and groom.

Explain that all of the cards will be placed into a folder and presented to the bride and groom later this evening; however, we will be sharing 'the best of the advice' just before we are ready to start part two of the evening.

Distribute the cards among the tables of guests and urge them to complete them in the next fifteen minutes. Provide pens or pencils as required. Remind them every five minutes until you are ready to collect the cards.

What actually happens is that people will bring you their cards once completed, especially those which are a little rude or close to the bone. This is where you need to be responsible and to edit the cards for public consumption. You will have already agreed guidelines beforehand with your bride and groom.

Once you have collected the cards and selected about ten to twenty examples you are ready to share them with the audience. Ideally you will have a mix of content: sincere, humorous and some a little rude.

Position the bride and groom on the dance floor or at a nearby table and step out with a radio microphone.

I found it best to ask whose name was on the card first. "First one up is from Uncle Arthur; where are you?" The reason for this is that people will now know who Uncle Arthur is and where he is sitting. I may go one step further and ask Uncle Arthur to read what he has written, especially if I am not sure as to how well received the message will be. Alternatively I may ask a guest whether this advice is something which works for them.

There are a few traps to avoid, the main one being that it is not unknown for someone to sign a card on behalf of someone else so that when you read a person's name they go red-faced and realise someone on their table has played a trick.

The beauty of this living guest book is that it focuses attention on the bride and groom at a time which is normally quite quiet. It works on two levels by introducing guests to the audience as a whole, thereby identifying where the relatives are and the work colleagues or next door neighbour, etc. The other level reveals just what kind of people they are and often reveals situations or events we would otherwise not know about.

I would recommend finishing with a couple of sincere pieces of advice from mum and dad and then invite a warm round of applause for the bride and groom for being good sports. Finally I would remind those guests whose cards were not read out that they will still be found in the presentation folder. Beware that next time you are invited round for coffee the folder may well be produced and those comments may come back to bite them!

Simply the best party pack

Sometimes a bride will say something like, "I want a fun party with everyone on the dance floor." Easy to say but not easy to achieve as many a DJ has found to his cost. This was my answer. Again, I should stress that this will not be to everyone's taste. When I first had this idea shared with me I thought, "No way, not at a wedding reception". However, I am happy to say I was wrong. What follows is a description of a type of interaction which can only be explained as explosive. When deployed correctly it is almost like turning on a switch.

Simply the best party pack is a 'party in a box'. For me this is an add-on option, meaning I charge the client for the service.

If they agree I would find out what they thought would be a good idea to include; for example, if they were going on a honeymoon to Hawaii, I would go out and buy a selection of coconut bras, leis and grass skirts as well as novelty items like inflatable guitars, saxophones and microphones together with tambourines, maracas and a selection of party hats and glittery boppers and wands.

Now there is nothing unique about using inflatable props and stuff to add a bit of fun to a party; however, in our case it was 'the way which we used them' which gave us our desired result. We would insist that all of these items were kept a secret. Only the bridal party was aware of them. We would begin the evening reception in the usual way and gently build the atmosphere as we approached the time for the bride and groom's first dance. The first dance would be as romantic and personal as we could make it. We would still encourage the addition of a father / daughter dance or maybe a 'family' dance. Either way, up to and including the end of these dances, nobody would have a clue as to what was about to happen.

Imagine the surprise and mayhem which erupted as I played a high energy track like 'La Bamba' while inviting the guest "to join our party" as an army of helpers including venue staff, bridesmaids and groomsmen helped distribute the party pack among the guests. Mature booted and suited men would have an air guitar thrust into their hands. Women would be given their beachcomber hat and maracas. Guys could be seen wearing their sun glasses and 'Blues Brothers fedoras'. The music would continue with a set of, dare I say, cheesy party tunes. A Blues Brothers medley would be followed by 'Surfing USA', 'Rockin' all over the world', 'Let's twist again' and requests generated from the guests which would by now be going crazy. I have video to prove it.

It never failed to ignite the room and create a frenzy activity on the dance floor. The sight of all the guests adorned with Hawaiian leis and all those props was amazing. Instantly people became aware that this was a fun party. It was a celebration in every sense of the word. We took no prisoners; everybody had to have a good time and they did!

I still don't fully understand why this worked so well. Logic would say that it wouldn't. My fear was the guests would shy away and refuse to accept the props as they were offered them, but they didn't.

I guess the best analogy I could think of, which I used when explaining the concept to potential clients, was that of a family Christmas meal. What makes a Christmas meal so different from any other meal?

It's probably the Christmas crackers, which make a bang when pulled and reveal their contents. The family wears their silly hats and reads the corny jokes found inside while trying to make out what novelty gift flew over the other side of the table. The seasonal music is playing and before you know it everyone is in the moment and enjoying the occasion.

And last but by no means least – the love story

You may have heard about this on the internet or in DJ forums. This is where you act as a narrator and tell the story of how the bride and groom met, fell in love, and found themselves at the venue on this, their wedding day. Usually the 'love story' is presented just before the bride and groom take to the floor for their first dance. Done well this can be the highlight of the day. Done badly this can be embarrassing.

Generally I would say 99.9 % of DJs cannot do this without formal training. A good 'love story' can only be told by a close friend, someone who is sincere and who understands the emotions involved. In a nutshell the DJ who undertakes a 'love story' needs talent in so many skills. He or she needs to be a good listener and a good writer, as well as a confident orator.

The 'love story' can be incredibly powerful and indeed may be your unique selling point. If you are interested in learning how to do this I would suggest you seek out the husband and wife team who created it and made it their signature piece.

Mark and Rebecca Farrell: www.Markferrell.com

Once again I cannot stress strongly enough that these suggestions are not a catalogue of activities to be rolled out in front of all your clients. You should explore your bride's vision and get to know her and the groom.

You need to understand what is acceptable to them and then if appropriate you may suggest one or two ideas which you think are suitable. The delivery has to be in accordance with your client's personality and the atmosphere they requested. Do not fall into the trap of packing too much into one party. Remember, less is more. The bride and groom only require one good reason to book you.

10] STAGING

This may come across as an unusual subject to purist DJs who do little more than play music and make the occasional announcement. Staging is about setting a scene. It involves coordination of people and their movements. Sometimes it is better to dismantle and separate elements rather than have them all bundled together.

Take a simple buffet meal. What happens when a buffet is opened without staging? Inevitably one of two things will happen. Either the announcement falls on deaf ears and nobody responds or there is a mad dash resulting in a free-for-all. Wouldn't it be so much better to plan a way of directing people to the buffet in a more controlled and orderly fashion?

I would suggest that it would be so much better if the whole process was stage managed like this. Play a rousing piece of music or custom jingle to grab attention and then make an announcement inviting the bride and groom to open the buffet. You will have previously made sure they were willing to do this and that they were ready and waiting for you to begin the 'opening'. Next you would invite the bridal party to join the bride and groom at the buffet table. Once again they would have been fully briefed as to what was going to happen earlier.

It may also be prudent to explain that remaining guests will be invited to the buffet table on a table-by-table rota. You will need to be diplomatic and point out why you are doing things this way. Explain the benefits of not having to wait in line for longer than necessary. The guests will be served more quickly and not to worry as there is plenty of food for everyone.

The end result is a controlled process where everybody is informed and included in the process. The venue management will appreciate this and the serving of the food will be quicker because the focus was shifted from the music to the food and the bride and groom.

The first dance

Let's take a look at a first dance introduction and see how staging can make a difference to the outcome. By difference I really mean impact or flow of the proceedings. If there was no staging then I guess there would be an announcement and the bride and groom would already be on the dance floor. The music would start and people close by would get to see what was happening.

After the first dance another piece of music would be played and the remaining guests invited to join the bride and groom on the dance floor. That is, if the bride and groom do not walk off after their first dance. How can we better stage manage this part of the evening?

When we stage a part of the evening it is to ensure maximum exposure. We are setting what is about to happen apart from what has preceded this and whatever is to follow. The staging creates a moment which is memorable and unique; without staging it could just get lost among the crowd and be over and done with without notice.

So how do we stage a bride and groom's first dance?

It's up to you; there are many ways to do it. I will give you one example to give you an idea. Go to YouTube and you will see hundreds of examples.

Good staging requires preparation and planning. You do not want to leave anything to chance. You will require help to stage a memorable first dance. If you have an assistant so much the better; if not, you may need the help of a best man or bridesmaid.

First I would arrange for the bride and groom to be taken out of the room or placed as far away from the dance floor as possible. If they are outside make sure the doors are closed and nobody can see them. I would have previously explained when the first dance was going to take place and I would have given five-minute warnings leading up to the time agreed upon.

Again I would precede my announcement with a fanfare or lively instrumental. The volume would rise and if possible I would change the lighting thereby utilising two senses to help attract attention. I would make the announcement using their Christian and surnames, making it personal to them. The assistant would open the doors at the correct time or prompt the bride and groom to walk forward through the crowd. The music would be adding to the excitement and the volume lowered once they reach the dance floor.

Keep your announcement short and sweet. Do not use redundant phrases. Anything which is unnecessary to what is happening should be omitted from your announcement. Sometimes it can be a nice touch to have a microphone to hand and invite the groom to say a few words of thanks prior to his first dance. This will have been agreed earlier and done well it will appear to be spontaneous and natural. Whichever way you agree to do things the outcome will be pre-determined.

Some brides and grooms wish to dance throughout their dance entirely alone. Others want to start off alone but be joined by their family as soon as possible. If the bridal party are to join them a minute or two into the track make sure they are all in the loop and in position around the dance floor. Preferably introduce them by name so that other guests will know who they are. Finally invite the remaining guests to join the family on the dance floor to complete the process and achieve the result of a full dance floor as agreed.

Finally, Derek would like to share with you a real introduction which he and his wife, Carol, produced for a young couple shortly after he realised the importance of staging. I have changed their names but everything else is as was.

Jason and Anne

We had met with Jason and Anne and they had decided to do things differently at their wedding. They were to be married in church and would have their wedding reception at a local four-star hotel. We would be with them all day starting with background music for their drinks reception on arrival at the hotel and later at the wedding breakfast in the main function suite.

They had decided to have their speeches and toasts first. They were also planning on using the base of their wedding cake as dessert for the meal. It was therefore essential that the cake was cut before or during the meal so that the staff could prepare the cake for serving. They also said they wanted a party atmosphere during the day and not to have to wait until the evening guests arrived before they could let their hair down. The party was to begin the moment they entered to room.

Their choice of music for their 'grand entrance' was 'It must be love' by Madness. More importantly, we decided they would step into the room immediately the first words of "It must be love, love, love" were heard. This is actually some fifty seconds into the instrumental opening of the track. My challenge was to time my introduction so that everyone knew what was about to happen and deliver maximum impact, energy and dynamics into the room.

No pressure then!

This is how it went down.

The guests had been seated and the main doors closed. I was inside playing background music while my wife was outside with Jason and Anne. Secretly we had arranged with the duty manager for him to have his waiting staff stand in a line between the entrance and the cake table. They had bottles of champagne ready to 'pop' as the couple passed down the line. I started the track and using the intro as a bed, gradually raising the volume, I explained that the bride and groom had decided to cut their cake before taking their seat at the top table prior to introductions, speeches and the meal. "Ladies and gentlemen, please be upstanding and welcome into the room your bride and groom, Jason and Anne Birchall."

The words "It must be love, love, love" sailed across the guests as the doors flew open and they stepped into the room. Everyone was on their feet clapping and cheering. The champagne corks went pop, pop, pop as they passed the line of waiters and eventually arrived at the cake.

The volume was lowered as I invited guests to join John and Anne at the cake table where they proceeded to cut the cake as I talked them through the cake cutting ceremony before finally taking their places at the top table. The rest of the day, needless to say, was filled with laughter and high spirits. We had more surprises in store for the guests but that, as they say, is another story.

I can't tell you how proud I was of that piece of staging. No doubt my description will not do it justice. I very seldom blow my own trumpet but on this occasion I make no apologies. The self-satisfaction of turning their vision into a reality which touched everyone in the room was amazing. I had never had a buzz like that simply playing music in the evening. At that moment in time I knew there was a better way to use my talent. You can do it too. You have the skills and the knowledge; maybe you just need the inspiration. There are many people out there who are prepared to help you. I found them and with the help of this book you can find them too.

It is difficult in a book to illustrate the importance of staging. Staging is a physical and visual medium and does not lend itself easily to the written word. Reading a script is one thing. Making note of the producer's direction notes is difficult until you get into the rehearsal room or onto the stage. However, staging is very important when we consider 'how' we do things as DJs. A good DJ will understand that music and his voice alone are not enough to guarantee creating a memorable moment.

Simply by adding some staging and production to what is happening will help you reach that higher level and produce amazing moments.

I would strongly recommend you take a look at the work of Randy Bartlett's 1% solution series of training DVDs. Randy has gone to great lengths to film many aspects of staging as well as illustrating how you can take what you do now to the next level.

You may have some concerns with regard to content, especially as everything is based on American weddings. Some of the stuff will not be of use but believe me when I tell you that most of it is invaluable and certainly can be applied to a wedding anywhere in the world. http://www.dj1percentsolution.com/

11] INVESTING IN YOURSELF

Generally, most mobile DJs are self-taught. We learnt by our mistakes; at least, I did. I shudder to think at what cost to our clients. We screwed up at someone's party so that we could learn and become better? Ignorance is bliss and I guess because we didn't charge much and had proper day jobs it all seemed okay. We used to come across other DJs in local hotels or pubs and looked at what they were doing. If we saw something we liked we would copy it. Sadly, it appears in most cases little has changed over the last 25 years. I still meet DJs who are repeating this same process.

Forums

How can you take advice from someone you don't know and who doesn't identify themselves? Forums can be a good place to seek advice; however, I would qualify this by pointing out that advice should only be taken from those you know and trust. Unfortunately, many people who post on forums do not reveal their true identity and it can be difficult to sort the wheat from the chaff.

You can suffer information overload on some forums and the advice given can often be contradictory. My advice would be to find a forum you are comfortable with and establish a rapport with a few DJs who you trust, ideally having met them in real life. Forums are good at communicating the latest news about products and events. Look out for meetings of DJs and get yourself along. There is no substitute for face-to-face conversation, especially if you are seeking advice. Check out the information provided by Ian Forrest and Darren Thomas.

Disc jockey associations

The idea of an association is based on mutual assistance. Most sectors of business and professional organisations have associations. In some circumstances these associations are compulsory where membership is a sign of accreditation and competence. Perception is reality and belonging to an association in some clients' eyes indicates a commitment to professionalism. This is something you may bear in mind when joining an association. Just using their logo and your membership details on your marketing materials can lift you above the competition in the mind of the potential client.

Usually membership of an association will require you to adhere to a code of practice and a minimum level of business integrity. This will require you to have public liability insurance and to provide proof that all of your equipment is in good order, is regularly maintained and is safe to use. This alone will not make you a better DJ but it will give potential clients confidence when making enquiries with you.

Education plays a big part of what most associations provide for their members. Many have dedicated forums. They also arrange meetings on a regular basis. These meetings will help DJs to get to know their colleagues / competitors and to build professional relationships. Meetings often feature latest product demonstrations either by manufacturers or supporting retailers.

Technical knowledge is never far away and there are plenty of members who are willing to share their experience so that you can avoid making the same mistakes they did in the past. Formal training is also starting to emerge via disc jockey associations. Recently I have noticed a range of topics being offered covering almost every aspect of our craft. Associations will often lend their support to trade shows and exhibitions in addition to providing special in-house events.

DJAA (Australia):

The DJ Alliance Australia is a committee of professional DJ entertainers from around Australia who joined forces to create a quality benchmark for their industry. As a client, it gives them peace of mind that when they hire an accredited DJAA member they can be assured of quality. All members adhere to a code of ethics and go through a number of reference checks before being approved as a member. Becoming a member of the DJ Alliance of Australia not only gets you accredited but links you with like-minded professionals across Australia. The process is designed to help grow your business and give you the opportunities to step up along the way. Most importantly, the DJAA sets out minimum standards you must meet to proceed to the next level. The Alliance is all about helping the industry as a whole and if this is something you would like more info on visit their website www.djaa.com.au

BPM Show in England:

This show is held at the NEC in Birmingham once a year in October. It has grown steadily over the years and is now the largest DJ show in the UK and probably Europe and the world depending on which statistic these things are measured by. BPM is a joint venture between Mark Walsh and Eddie Short. Eddie is the editor of Pro Mobile magazine and both of these guys work tirelessly to bring together the very latest and best in DJ products, entertainment and education. This is a one-stop shop for DJs who want to keep in touch with the DJ world. Here you can see the world's foremost DJ talent showcased alongside the latest equipment and you also have the opportunity to be part of three days of learning in the custom seminar suites. Investing in a ticket for BPM is a no-brainer; every DJ should go at least once.

National Association of Disc Jockeys – NADJ (England):

NADJ support the BPM show and representatives are on hand to explain the benefits of membership. Their members can often be found in the seminar rooms presenting information and advice on a number of topics. The association will also support its local branches around the country by providing visits from manufacturers and retailers together with presentations on issues which affect their members. NADJ is constantly seeking new members and locations for branch meetings. If there is no local branch in your area you could easily set one up. It only takes a handful of members to organise their own branch. You set the agenda and select a venue and representatives from the national committee will support you.

South Eastern Disc Jockey Association – SEDA:

The guys and girls from the south east of England meet regularly in and around Maidstone in Kent. This long-established and flourishing association is an ideal place to learn and network. SEDA produce an excellent 'show night' experience where they bring together industry leaders and 'showcase' latest products. SEDA also support BPM and are also on hand to meet new and prospective members. They also contribute to the educational seminars. Although based in the south east of the country membership is not limited to this area. Indeed, membership is not limited to any one association; some DJs belong to two or more.

Other groups and associations:

I apologise for not specifically mentioning any of the other groups or associations that may exist. I can only comment on and recommend those associations, groups and individuals I have personal experience of. New groups are forming all the time. This is both good news and bad news. Good because these groups are filling a need for their members but the down side is that they fragment what is already out there.

Why reinvent the wheel? IF only DJs could work under one umbrella association they would have a better chance of recognition by the general public and the industry they seek to represent. "United we stand, divided we fall!" I see no reason why individual associations can't maintain their own identities and manage the day-to-day running of their associations whilst existing under one banner. Maybe one day in the future this may happen but I will not be holding my breath.

Trade publications

There are a number of magazines which promote DJs and are targeted at our market. Once again I can only recommend the two I have subscribed to and which I believe best represent the mobile DJ wishing to specialise in weddings.

Pro Mobile magazine:

To my knowledge this is the only magazine in the UK specifically dedicated to operators of mobile discos. The editor, Eddie Small, is a mobile DJ himself and he understands the industry very well. Eddie has travelled abroad extensively and gathered together an eclectic mix of contributors to write for his magazine. The articles are informative, educational and often amusing. The product reviews are full of facts and practical explanations written without too much jargon in a style we can all understand. Pro Mobile magazine is also supported by some top-class retailers and manufacturers whose advertisements keep us abreast of new products and special offers. It is a 'must read' for any mobile DJ, and guess what, you can subscribe online and they will post to Australia.

Mobile Beat magazine:

This is an American publication which you can subscribe to and receive by mail in the UK and Australia or conveniently it can be read online at their website. Derek first came across this magazine while on holiday in North Carolina back in 1998. This is in the days before Pro Mobile and at that time they did not have a similar magazine in the UK.

I discovered it through the university YouTube and Brian S. Redd. What? A magazine for mobile DJs? I subscribed as soon as I found out and looked forward to each of the issues with excitement. I would read them from cover to cover and back again. They were, and are, packed with articles and features, technical and practical, covering the whole gamut of issues faced by mobile DJs. I am delighted by the magazine; they are piled up in cupboards all around the house, to my wife's disgust. But I still go back and use them as a reference now and then and I get so frustrated that no such magazine exists over here in Australia. Maybe someone could take on the challenge and start a simple online subscription version for us Aussies; I'm sure if someone asked Ryan or Eddie for help they would jump at it.

The Mobile Beat magazine also hosted a trade show, or convention, for its readership. Actually back then it held two such events each year: one in the winter and the other in the summer. The winter event took place in Las Vegas while the summer event was held in a different location each year. The main attraction to me was that alongside the exhibit wall where all the 'boys' toys' were available there was an extensive seminar area and a full three days of educational content provided by well-respected American and Canadian DJs. I just had to go and see this, which I did eventually in 2002. I can honestly say I'm now a better DJ, MC and entertainer.

I earn five to six times more now than before I attended the Mobile Beat DJ show in Las Vegas; it truly changed my life. It's similar to the BPM shows in England. Spend time investing in you. I highly recommend it.

Mobile Beat DJ convention

I had no real idea what to expect. I just knew that I wanted to sit in the seminar rooms and listen. I needed to find out how DJing differed from what we do in Australia or did we do the same things? It turned out that we often do the same things only differently. However, what I did learn was that in many ways the Americans were years ahead of us in terms of professionalism and customer service. Two areas I am particularly interested in. Imagine how I felt as a lone Aussie seated in a room full of about 1000 DJs?

I later found out that I was not the only foreigner in the hall. There were guys from Africa, England, Mexico, Ireland and Canada who I met while I was there. In fact, the hospitality was amazing. I remember standing outside the foyer of the Riviera on our first day with my wife. We were chatting about our experience since arriving. There was a group of about a dozen guys close to us who were obviously DJs. One of them overheard our conversation and simply asked where we were from. When he found out we were from Australia he was blown away; within minutes we were invited to join the group and ended up spending the evening with them. We were inundated with questions about how we DJ down under. I had lots of questions for them too. They also started sharing ideas and writing down details about this and that and we left for our room armed with scraps of paper and business cards with contact details. The next day I remember standing in the queue to buy Randy Bartlett's video, again just complete strangers asking each other where we were from. When from a distance I heard someone say, "Is that an Aussie accent I hear?" in an Australian accent. It was Robert who was a DJ from my home town Melbourne: my competition; we lived 40 minutes away from each other and never met until we were in Vegas. I'm honoured to now be friends with him and we often refer clients to each other when we are booked. Las Vegas is an amazing place to visit at any time of the year, let alone to attend a DJ convention. You never know who you might meet.

Over the following three days I learnt so much. I travelled to the USA thinking there was not that much to learn; after all, I had been DJing at parties for the best part of 20 years. How wrong was I. "You just don't know what you don't know."

The seminar 'Getting what you're worth' by Mark Ferrell was to change my entire perception of what I was doing as a mobile DJ. Later I met Mark and his wife Rebecca and signed up to his private forum which was then called Disc Jockey America. This was the beginning of an ongoing collaboration which saw me return to the convention a second time two years later and I discovered the MarBecca Method workshops.

Mobile Beat is also where I met some of the nicest and inspiring people I know like Peter Merry, Randy Bartlett, Jim Cerone, Larry Williams, Tom Haibeck, Scott Faver and Ryan Burger These gentlemen are major providers of educational content in the USA. Some of their work has been made available to us either directly from the author, their websites or via online book stores.

The rest, as they say, is history. I would urge you, dear reader, to take a similar leap of faith and visit this amazing event. The cost of the trip is a legitimate business expense as is the investment in educational materials or workshops. How do you fancy a week in Las Vegas? Take what you do to the next level and reap the rewards both financially and professionally.

The show is held every February. Flights are reasonable and accommodation and food are cheap. The show is now a four-day event starting on Monday and finishing on Thursday. I would recommend that you have a couple of days either side to relax. Therefore travelling Saturday to Saturday is a good idea. This means sacrificing two Saturdays out of your diary but in reality you will get that back in no time with what you gain from attending.

Expect to pay about $1300 return for your flight and $700 for your hotel although some companies like Expedia can often offer packages. Prices are fluid and travel costs vary according to when you book. Look out for special offers which come and go without any recognisable trend. Best to check regularly with the airlines and be ready to snap up a bargain when offered.

Your show pass which gets you into all four days of the convention and the parties associated with it will cost around $130 if booked before the end of December. There may also be discounts for early purchasers. The later you leave it the more expensive this pass becomes. Check out their website for full details. www.mobilebeat.com

ArmDJs – Robbie Britton

If you are looking for an educational programme in the winter months and would like to combine it with a week's holiday in a beautiful historic part of America, look no further.

This event takes place over a couple of days in June and is located in Johnson City, Tennessee. The host, Robbie Britton, is a charming, unassuming family man who has created a very successful entertainment company which provides a diverse range of services in what I would describe as rural America.

Much of the educational content is provided by the same high-quality presenters you would find at the Mobile Beat show. However, this show feels more relaxed and less hurried. A point worth bearing in mind is that there is only one seminar at a time being presented so you will not miss a thing. If you have doubts about visiting Las Vegas this show provides a complete contrast while still producing top-notch education.

While in Tennessee take time out to visit Nashville, the home of country music; you couldn't travel all that way without visiting 'Graceland', the home of Elvis Presley, which is situated in Memphis. Every mobile DJ will have played Elvis's music at some time or other. This visit will be an education in itself. Seeing his costumes and the gold and platinum discs, which pay testament to the 'King', adorning the walls of his house is amazing!

You could also make your way up into the Smoky Mountains and visit Gatlinburg which is not too far away from Dolly Parton's 'Dollywood' theme park.

So if you're looking to combine business with pleasure this may be your cup of tea. Remember all costs and expenses related to education and training can be offset against tax.

Getting there is not so easy. There are no direct flights and you will need to hire a car. However, this show comes highly recommended. Meanwhile if you need more information drop Robbie a line via the website and say hi. http://www.armdjs.com

Some of you may be put off because these are American shows and the material is also American. I have met many DJs who switch off at the mention of all things American. Usually this is because they disagree with American culture or business ethics or maybe they see Americans as insincere. I can honestly say I had no such doubts.

Yes, I had a stereotypical image of Americans when I first visited Las Vegas but I soon realised my misconceptions were unfounded. Yes, you have to cut through the crap and the hype. Underneath you will find quality content which is of use and value to you and your business. There are many successful American businesses operating in Australia. We can and do learn a great deal from them. My own earning potential rose as a result of what I learnt from Americans. Don't allow an unfounded prejudice to cloud your judgement.

You may know of a British DJ by the name of Alan Marshall. He too found his way over to the United States. He found it all by himself. He made the connection and is now embarked on his own journey. This journey is taking him along a similar path to the one I chose. He is upping his game and raising the bar as indeed are a number of DJs all around the world. You will find some of their stories among these pages.

Now I know there are a lot of sceptical DJs out there who believe that they know all they need to know. I guess that does not include you as why else would you be reading this book? There are many DJs who will tell you that a wedding DJ only needs a great sound and light show and that the success of the event is down to the music played. These DJs will say that interaction is cheesy and only a repeat of what we did in the seventies and eighties. They diminish everything they hear about Americans to the lowest possible denominator and make assumptions which are not based on fact. If we take American ideas and then translate them into a format and style which is acceptable to the Australian public we will be bringing more options to our clients. Once again I repeat,

"Your client doesn't know what they don't know."

Workshops

A workshop is not a seminar. Generally a seminar is mainly a lecture with the possibility of a little interaction with the audience. Usually the amount of interaction is restricted by the numbers of those attending and the agenda set by the presenter. A workshop is more hands-on. It is in such an environment that you can get involved and practise what is being taught. Sharing of information is not just two-way as the attendee will also learn from others who attend the workshop. Think of a workshop as a coaching session and you are halfway there. All professionals need a coach. Sportsmen and actors regularly attend coaching sessions. Businessmen and women are often sent on training courses by their employers.

There are always new ideas or new technology which help make our lives better or easier. Keeping abreast of change and stretching to achieve higher standards will pay dividends eventually.

Alas, there are not many DJ-specific workshops to be found on this side of the world. I have been known to organise some around the country with limited success. I am sure there will be more experienced DJs who will share their knowledge in this way. Look out for them. Elsewhere you will most probably be able to find workshops covering related subjects like web design, social networking, acting classes or a stand-up comedy class which I would recommend you take advantage of. Many of these are relatively inexpensive and some are even free. Check out your local library or council offices for such activity in your area.

This whole book is about options and choices. We have a choice to stay doing what we always did, and get back in return what we always got.

Only a few months ago I met a DJ who I used to work for and he still runs a multi-operator DJ business. And he said to me he could not get any more for his services now than he did 10 years ago. After some questioning I saw he was still doing the same things he was doing 10 years ago! Have you heard this before? He doesn't know what he doesn't know! He actually believes he is the best mobile DJ in Melbourne, and can't see past his nose. I tried to help him, inviting him to invest in himself, not just his equipment, without any luck. (I'm going to send him a copy of this book.)

So we can evolve and bring more to the party other than music. Yes, music is still important but so too is entertainment and inclusion.

We owe it to our clients and their guests to offer something different. Corporate clients are always on the lookout for new activities. Brides are looking for a 'wow' factor, something not seen at any of their friends' weddings.

You could be that 'something different'.

12] THE COMPETITION

In order to stand out from the hundreds of disc jockeys in your area you need to understand who your competition is. It is also important for you to have in-depth knowledge of what they do and how they conduct themselves. Inevitably potential clients will try to compare you to others. "I can get the same thing elsewhere" or "But Mr DJ down the road will do it for $xxx" or other common retorts from those seeking our services.

You wouldn't be a very successful car salesman if you didn't have a good knowledge of the other makes and models available. Most people who are thinking of buying a car will be armed with a collection of brochures and will have test-driven some of the models which they think they would like. In theory you are unique and therefore there is no competition or comparison to be made; however, this is only true once you have established your uniqueness in your client's mind.

Disclaimer

What follows is my personal view of the competition in general which DJs up and down the country face day in, day out. You will no doubt disagree with some of the content. There will be exceptions to the rule and if anyone is offended by my comments I apologise. There are good and bad in all walks of life and I see no reason why things should be any different in the mobile DJ business. The important message for you to understand is that not all is as it seems, particularly to potential customers when they contact some of the other operators in the marketplace. So what are we up against out there?

Comparison of prices

You will find a wide range of prices for DJs in Australia. This key is designed to give you an idea of what is out there, from my understanding as a DJ in Melbourne for over 20 years.

$350-$600: More than likely this is a DJ company who sends out many DJs every weekend. Often these are DJs who have very little experience. These DJs are making $25-$30 an hour to DJ your wedding, with the company keeping the rest.

$700-$1000: These DJs are usually single-system companies, meaning they only have one DJ. These DJs have professional sound equipment, have years of experience and are talented, professional DJs, but may not have a good understanding of what's required to be a great Master of Ceremonies.

$1500+: These are the equivalent of luxury cars of DJs. These DJs do things that the other DJs don't do, like full custom intros for the entire bridal party (usually three to four sentences about each person in the bridal party) and custom produce songs, among other custom elements.

Where do you fit in?

Now that you have an idea of what a DJ costs, how do you choose which level you want to be in? At this point it's up to you to determine how much time you want to spend in the planning of a wedding reception and what level of personalisation you want to give your client. Do you just want to play music? Or be the DJ that will customise an event in terms of working with the client on what they would like to happen and then offer unique and creative suggestions for their reception (introductions, cake cutting, etc.).

Summary
Tier 1 ($350-$600): Limited or no mic or MC skills, no planning, no direction, very little experience, may not give any announcements, no professional training, little understanding of wedding etiquette or protocol.

Tier 2 ($600-$1000): Approximately less than five years' experience as a wedding DJ, some professional training, over 200 weddings performed. Offer very little planning, not able to meet with client at their convenience, decent mic and MC skills.

Tier 3 ($1500+): Many years of experience, has professional training as a Master of Ceremonies, polished MC and mic skills, two or three planning sessions, coordinator, direction, unique ideas, able to read the crowd, program music well, very good pro-audio equipment. Always dressed appropriately, understands wedding etiquette and protocol. Abides by the law, has public liability insurance and a PPCA permit. High standards.

Now I'm not saying that a $600 DJ is not good, conversely, that doesn't mean a $2000 DJ is the best; however, they will put a lot of work into the planning of the reception, most likely meeting with clients two or three times before the wedding for consultations. Although they may be in demand and talented, they may not suit the vibe of every reception.

You see, a DJ/MC will charge the fee they think they are worth. It's the demand and supply principle. If they don't get bookings then they lower the price until the bookings come. This also works the other way. If they are booked out every Saturday night and have to knock back clients, then they may decide that they are too cheap and the price goes up.

Single operator independent DJ

He or she will be the most easily understood and to make comparisons with. This DJ will be visible for you to call on the phone or maybe to meet at a multi-room venue. Marketing material will be specific featuring a biography. Usually there will be a website enabling you to get a good impression of where he or she has positioned their DJ service within the market. In other words you will get a pretty good impression based on what you know about being a mobile DJ and what you see in their marketing material and the prices they charge for their services.

Single-operator mobile DJs will often have a reputation locally. Good or not so good, excellent or average, you need to know as much as possible about this type of competitor, especially their strengths and weaknesses. The single operator will usually turn down a booking if that date is already filled. He may suggest a choice of DJs he knows that would be suitable. He or she prides themselves on being independent and guaranteed to attend the contracted booking.

Multi-operator

The multi-operator has usually started out as a one-man band and has expanded to cover increased demand for his services. He could have increased his prices but decided to increase supply instead. So now his company has duplicated what it does and offers a selection of DJs to its clients. This is often a situation which gets a little cloudy in clients' eyes.

Does the company offer named individual DJs or do they select from an anonymous staff list? Does their client receive a contract naming an individual DJ? Do they get to meet that DJ as part of the booking and planning process? Are the DJs supplied by the multi-operator employed by them or are they sub-contracted? More importantly, are the DJs exclusive to the company or are they available elsewhere? Are they, as is often the case, single operators who are seeking work by sub-contracting to the multi-operator?

In a nutshell can a client be certain of what they are getting from a multi-operator? Do they get a guarantee that the DJ who turns up to perform at their wedding is as experienced and fully informed as a single-operator DJ would be?

DJ agencies

There is a fine line between the multi-operator and the DJ agency. I am not talking here about general entertainment agencies. The DJ-specific agencies most probably started out in the same way as the multi-ops. They made the decision not to try and duplicate what they did based upon their image and experience. They decided to capitalise on the increased demand for supplying a disco. They figured there are loads of DJs out there seeking work and they had the enquiries to fill. DJ agencies can be a win-win for the client. The agency provides a one-stop opportunity to gather information and be given a choice of DJ based upon their needs. The agent simply matches those needs and negotiates a contract usually, but not always, between the client and the DJ.

The agency will charge a fee for his service that the DJ is happy to pay as this avoids him or her from having to market themselves or deal with any administration. In some instances the agent will contract themselves to the client and then arrange a separate contract with the DJ. This usually happens when the agent collects the full fee and then passes the agreed amount, less commission, to the DJ. Once again there are advantages and disadvantages for both parties. I only mention the contractual issues so that you may seek specific information from DJ agencies that you know operate in your area. Knowing what they do and how they do it and who they supply will be vital in your objective in identifying the difference between you and them.

Entertainment agencies

Entertainment agencies will offer a whole range of service providers. They are very often members of an association and abide by a code of conduct which makes dealing with them transparent and uncomplicated. These agencies are often the preferred choice of hotel groups and prestigious venues because they are a one-stop shop for all of their entertainment needs. These agencies can be very selective as to who they promote and will often have very high standards which potential service providers will have to meet if they are to be featured by these agents. Generally it is in the agent's best interests to promote you and to attain the highest possible fee in return for your services.

The more they charge, the more you earn. Usually their commission will be a straight percentage of the fee charged to a client. Typically agents will take fifteen to twenty percent of the fee. Some single-operator DJs will also seek work from this type of agent. There should be no conflict of interest here if the process remains true and transparent. However, not all agents are as professional as others and some may seek the opportunity to make more money off the back of the service provider. Take care to ensure that the slice of the cake is in the right proportion. It is not uncommon to find an agent taking the biggest piece of pie while leaving you with the crumbs.

Once again I would reiterate that these are my personal observations. Not all companies portray themselves in a transparent way. What appears to be a single DJ could well turn out to be a multi-op or agent. Forewarned is forearmed when it comes to offering advice to clients and informing them of the level playing field which exists, or not, as the case may be.

Bands and artists who also 'DJ'

It is becoming increasing popular for other service providers to offer a package deal to their clients which include DJ services. Generally this would be a band or solo singer who agrees to do their usual performance slots but who will also 'fill-in' with a DJ set. On the face of it this can be an attractive alternative to the unsuspecting client. However, we know differently, don't we? I can safely say I have never seen an 'artist' who can DJ as well as an independent DJ. The very fact that they believe they can do both trivialises the talent and contribution made by the DJ. Usually the 'artist' considers they are more important than recorded music and that the DJ just gets in the way of their performance. If they DJ they are in control and their preference and taste prevail. I would always point out to potential clients the number of occasions when I have worked with a band who made me look great because they were, well, not so great. I could cite examples of numerous occasions when a member of the band, or even one of their road staff, took to playing a DJ set while the other members took a break. Not a good idea. We are the experts and this is our territory which is to be defended at all costs. Seek out these competitors in your area and be ready to 'tell it like it is' if required.

Resident DJs

The resident DJ situation is a double-edged sword. Many DJs aspire to have a residency while to others the resident DJ is the enemy. Being a resident DJ is a strange anomaly in the entertainment business. I am not talking about club DJs here because this is a book for mobile DJs who wish to target the wedding industry. A resident club DJ makes perfect sense because people will pay to be in his presence on the night he performs. I refer here mainly to hotels that employ a resident DJ or agency. Do hotels have a resident band? Do they have a resident singer? So how come they have a resident DJ? Probably the answer lies in a perverse logic which I am afraid to admit originated in the DJ's mind.

A singer or band or a photographer would not be willing or able to perform at a regular venue in return for a price which meant they could not afford to exist as professionals. They will gladly offer their services as preferred suppliers but they will retain control of the booking process either independently or via their agency. Unfortunately at some point in history mobile DJs decided it would be a good idea to hand over the booking process to the hotel and allow them to call the shots. The DJs were happy to dilute their fees in return for regular work and maybe being able to store equipment on site, effectively taking the mobile out of their service agreement.

This was all well and good as long as the hotel did not regard the DJ as a commodity. Alas, many DJs then proceeded to supply substitute DJs to the venue and the venue could no longer identify what was special about their original choice. The accounts department also ceased the opportunity to make money and increase their profit margins. So now the hotel charges a price which is in line with their status while the DJ receives what he is prepared to accept.

Let's not kid ourselves here. A hotel's biggest fear when it comes to providing a resident DJ is a 'no show'. If a DJ fails to turn up to a booking which they have arranged they will be in deep poo poo. To them the DJ is now a commodity and a service which surprisingly other DJs are keen to supply. You can guarantee every week a number of letters or phone calls are received by quality hotels from DJs who want to be their resident DJ. The rules of the marketplace are in the hotel's favour. Supply and demand dictates that the job goes to the lowest bidder and we find ourselves being the cheapest item on the menu.

To add insult to injury the situation is often exacerbated when it comes to being paid. Many hotels are part of groups or chains of companies which have complex administration systems. The service provider needs to ensure that he complies with the invoicing policy or he may be left waiting for his cash for weeks or even months. Some companies even insist that you pay a fee to be a supplier to their organisation.

"The multi-chain hotel and resident DJs are killing the mobile DJ!"
-Derek Pengelly

Derek knows what he is talking about. He used to be a resident DJ in a hotel. He has also supplied DJs to hotels as a resident multi-operator. And confesses to being one of those who has perpetuated this ridiculous situation.

Why did he do it? Probably for the same reasons as the people who are doing it today. No man is an island. He was simply responding to a market which already existed. Derek didn't create that market; he just decided he wanted to be a part of it. The vital point here is to understand what is happening in your locality. Check out just how much local hotels charge for a DJ. Then decide if you want to be a part of the resident DJ situation or if you would rather be independent. Use the price which they charge their customers as your starting point and then add value. People are not stupid and they will appreciate quality and be prepared to pay more for it. Do not be afraid to charge what you believe you are worth. Not everyone wants to buy cheap.

Preferred supplier (to a venue)

This is the smart option and the solution to the problem with venues that have a resident DJ who is effectively on their payroll, or better still, no resident DJ at all. Ideally a venue should have a list of preferred suppliers. These suppliers will have been vetted and proved themselves as professionals with whom the venue can work alongside and confidently recommend. Providing a choice is healthy. The hotel no longer carries any responsibility for providing the entertainment. The client will choose based upon what the supplier has to offer. No two DJs are the same and no two clients are either. The venue can now leave the administration to the supplier. All they require is a good working relationship and great communication. As long as they know about what you do and how you do it they will be content to let you do your thing. This removes the restraints on pricing and you can now offer your range of services and products depending upon the customer's requirements.

You are still in competition with other DJ preferred suppliers but at least you now have the opportunity to establish your worth and why the client should book you. In order to achieve this objective as a preferred supplier and take control of the booking process you may have to recompense the venue.

Some venues will be happy just to have less involvement whilst the accountants may be reluctant to lose a source of revenue. It may well be prudent to offer the hotel some form of retainer or commission based upon each confirmed booking or the final invoice amount. Indeed, some venues may have this arrangement in place before they invite you or agree to you becoming one of their preferred suppliers.

Closed-shop venues and restrictive clauses

Some venues who operate a resident DJ policy will insist that their client uses their DJ or at least pays their fee before they are allowed to bring in their own choice. Now I am not a solicitor but I am pretty certain that under law this is known as a restricted practice and is illegal. However, the law is one thing and reality is something else. When faced with this situation I would support my client in any way possible. Initially I would encourage them to call the bluff of the venue. Are they really prepared to lose a booking worth many thousands of dollars because of a $450 to $650 penalty clause which is potentially illegal? I think not! I have known situations where the venue has backed down or reduced the fee to one which has been acceptable to my client. I have also known clients who wanted me so badly that they just bit the bullet and paid the fee. If you like your client and want to work for them you may wish to consider discounting your fee in order to reduce the pain and complete the deal. It's a difficult situation but one which I am afraid is becoming more and more popular, especially with what I would describe as prestigious venues.

The DJ community

Finally I would like to take time out to step back and take a look at the overall situation we find ourselves in. The opportunities to sell our services are plentiful. Education is the key to overcoming the pricing policies we are faced with. Remember that a bride and groom do not know the full picture. I doubt if all DJs fully appreciate the current situation. Historically it is your fellow DJs who created this low price mentality. It is also true to say that the situation could be reversed overnight if all DJs agreed a minimum price or hourly rate for their services. Alas, this will never happen. I guess such a move would also be illegal; the beauty of providing a quality product or service lies within the value placed upon it by those seeking it. Price should never be the issue. Quality and value should be, and in the case of weddings, will be of more importance.

In order to succeed as a professional wedding DJ you effectively have to ignore what has gone on in the past.

You need to break away from the shackles imposed on you by less talented or professional DJs and venues that have ceased the opportunity to make a quick buck at your expense. Don't listen to those who tell you that you can't charge this or that amount. Listen to those already earning above average fees. Seek out those who are successful and learn from their experience. It will not be easy at first. You cannot go from low fees to top dollar overnight. Investing in education for yourself and your client will pay dividends in time.

Remember too that not all people are your clients. You can and should refuse opportunities if you believe that you cannot provide the right service. Saying no can sometimes be very therapeutic and will underpin your professionalism. Move on and concentrate on your next opportunity.

13] CONTRACTS

Contracts are difficult documents to write. Each DJ will want to protect his interests while the client should feel protected once they have signed it. Therefore any contract for services provided needs to be balanced and fair to both parties. There is no point in including terms and conditions which are unreasonable or biased. For example, while it may be desirable to want to hold a bride responsible for damage caused to your equipment at a party it is unreasonable for her to be expected to know what every guest is up to at all times. She is not responsible for their actions, they are. The best you can hope for is an obligation for her to divulge contact details for any such guest so that you may pursue them for compensation. The only other alternative would be to hold a deposit which is non-refundable if damage is caused.

Contracts will need to be worded differently if you are dealing directly with the general public or with a corporate body and / or a third party like an agent or event planner. Ideally you should seek legal advice. However, this is easier said than done, because there are very few solicitors experienced in entertainment and its complexities. Finding a suitable, qualified solicitor could be difficult and costly.

Trade associations may be able to help you. I believe the musician's union used to have a contract template and that the DJAA were working to produce one. However, a template is just the starting point. You will need to amend any such document to suit your requirements.

Contracts these days need to be transparent and once again less is more. Ideally you will never need to rely on enforcing a contract. In many instances you and your client will be insured and insurance can cover most situations. Incorporating a clear complaint procedure is probably your best course of action.

We used to insist that any complaint was brought to the DJ's attention, and our company representative, on the night of the performance. All too often it seems that clients can decide to complain after the event. Why this should be I have no idea. Sometimes it may be upon reflection or an issue is raised by a third party to the client without your knowledge. Most of what we do at parties is subjective so there is no way you can entertain comparisons with other entertainers' styles or content. Any complaint needs to be based on fact and not interpretation which is, by its very nature, subjective.

If you should receive a complaint the first thing you need to do is respond in a positive and concerned manner. Apologise for any upset or inconvenience but do not admit any liability at this stage. Ask for the complaint to be formally submitted in writing and advise your client of the time scale required to investigate the issue and respond. Often a simple "Sorry" and a token gesture of compensation is all that is required to settle a complaint. Do not take a complaint personally. This is business. Surprisingly, resolving a complaint speedily and satisfactorily can be good public relations.

I will share some examples of items which you may wish to include in your contract. Please feel free to use and amend these as you see fit. I would stress once again that the final document should be verified by a solicitor for it to be binding.

Deposits:

There is a school of thought which recommends that you do not use this terminology. It is suggested that this should be an 'initial payment' or 'part payment'. This is because a deposit does not necessarily reflect that the payment is made in respect of any service provided. Usually deposits are paid toward the purchase of goods. We provide a service and therefore it is suggested that the 'initial payment' covers your pre-event planning and meetings which can then be legitimately withheld should your client wish to cancel their contract. Once again, seek legal advice if you are uncertain.

While on the subject of 'deposits' let's take a look into why we take them and how much we should ask for. A deposit is taken as a gesture of good faith when a client signs a contract. I would suggest that the higher percentage of your fee which amounts to the deposit will be a better gesture than a smaller one. In other words, people may cancel a contract if they consider losing their deposit is not such a big deal. If on the other hand the deposit is a substantial amount of the total fee a client will think long and hard before cancelling.

Take a look at what is customary in the industry and fall in line with other service providers. I insisted on a deposit of one third of my fee. I know of others who required fifty percent. At the end of the day you must go with what you are comfortable with. Remember the deposit represents your pre-event work for which you need to be paid.

Deposits also have a major impact on your cash flow. When times are quiet it may well be that you increase your marketing activity.

Therefore if you are able to bank enough deposits it may well see you through times when you have no performances.

Final Payments:

You will notice that for weddings I would insist on the final payment being made two weeks before the event date. Again this is reasonable and customary in the wedding industry. There is nothing worse than trying to collect your fee on the day of the wedding. There are just too many areas of concern and situations which you do not want to get into. What if the person responsible for paying you spends your money before you have a chance to collect it? What if the cash you were promised turns out to be a cheque. Or worse still, what if the money was left at home? It is much better to have this issue sorted before the day of the wedding, especially as your client is covered by your contract. It also means they have one more thing not to worry about and can therefore relax and enjoy the day without having to worry about paying you.

In all circumstances I would insist that I needed to be paid once the equipment was set up and a sound check completed. This would be their last chance to honour their side of the contract. I had completed my obligation to be there and be ready to play music and I expected them to keep their side of the bargain. Otherwise the room would remain silent. Incidentally, I never had such an incident occur, thanks to my terms and conditions within the contract.

14] TESTIMONIALS

Testimonials are vital because they underpin and reinforce everything you say and do in your marketing materials, on your website and in your performances. There is nothing more powerful than a client or third party singing your praises. Human nature is such that if someone is happy about a product or service which they have purchased they will tell everyone who will listen. If you have exceeded their expectations they will be more than happy to recommend you to others. So how do we go about getting testimonials?

Obtaining testimonials is actually very simple; just ask for them!

For some reason most Australians are quite reserved and shy when it comes to asking for references. We would rather such testimonials were offered without prompting, and sometimes they are, but for your marketing plan to succeed you need to obtain as many as possible. There are many places a client can leave an online review: Google and Easy Weddings, just to name two. In my experience Facebook reviews get the most attention probably because of how easy it is for people to find and future clients can see a thumbnail of the face of the person that has left the review. If you don't have a FB business page I recommend you get on it fast because you are missing out.

Try to obtain a photograph of you and your clients on their wedding day showing them smiling and happy. Pictures speak a thousand words and images such as these will look great on your website. (Obtain permission before you publish them.) Video is also great for testimonials. Some videographers make a point of recording candid interviews with the bride and groom and their guests. Obtaining this footage will help you put together a montage which you can show to prospective clients.

In all instances I would recommend you send a paper questionnaire to your clients. This feedback form should be mainly a tick box exercise because people don't like filling in forms or answering long questions. I have included an example for you to consider using. I would also suggest that you include a stamped addressed envelope so that the document can be returned with the minimum of inconvenience. I found that almost ninety percent of these feedback forms were returned. You can, of course, send them via email but the return rate may not be so successful.

You will notice that within my feedback form we have kept the need to write comments to a minimum with two very important exceptions. As well as seeking praise for our services this document is designed to help you IMPROVE what you do and how you do it.

We can all make mistakes and even with the best-laid plans things will, and do, go wrong. What's important is the way you handle such situations and the way you respond. Turning a negative into a positive is a very powerful way to improve your business.

Don't forget to keep all of these documents and make them available for inspection. You may want to scan them and use them on your website or in brochures. Always make sure you have permission before you share any of this confidential information.

Your marketing materials tell the story of what you promise to provide for your clients.

Your testimonials will prove that you actually deliver all that you promise!

15] GOING THE EXTRA MILE

Outstanding performance and customer service is not easy to deliver. People have different levels of expectation and can be hard to please. This invariably means that as service providers we have to under-promise and over-deliver. We need to consistently exceed our clients' expectations. It all starts at that first point of contact and carries on to the moment you leave the venue at the end of the day. Actually it doesn't end there either!

Professionalism is not just what you do and how you do it, it's about your attitude, behaviour and passion. Demonstrating that you care about what you do and how you deliver your service is vital if you are to be perceived as a 'specialist wedding DJ'.

Many DJs say they specialise in weddings in their marketing materials but how many are truly 'expert' at what they do? So how do you demonstrate the right qualities and behaviour which will separate you from the others? What is it you need to do to establish yourself as a true professional?

Belief plays a big part in this process. You have to believe that you are good. You need to believe you are the best! You also need to tell everyone this fact. This is no time for modesty and anyway, how many DJs are modest about what they do? There is a fine line between confidence and arrogance so you need to tread carefully. However, if you do not proclaim yourself the best wedding specialist DJ in your area, who will? Having said that you better be able to back it up because if you don't word will spread quickly. I have often been told that I should blow my own trumpet more than I do. It's the way I am; however, I have learnt to be more forthright when it comes to dealing with clients and other service providers.

Does a bride want the second-best DJ in her area for her wedding entertainment? Does she want one of the best wedding DJs in the area to entertain her guests? Or would she rather be content and confident knowing she had booked the best wedding DJ in the area for her wedding? Brides have told me that they use the best in the search box when searching the internet for their wedding DJs. So include that word when next time you are reviewing your SEO.

Who is to say that you are NOT the best? Everything we do is subjective. It is almost impossible to prove or disprove such statements. How many times have you been told you were the best DJ at the end of a party? Did you believe them? Probably not.

Did they really mean it when they said it? Who knows? Who cares? How many 'best' Elvis tribute acts have you seen? In reality all that matters is that YOU believe you are the best and that you satisfy your client's expectations.

Attention to detail

It's the little things which can often make a big difference.

When Derek worked as a representative for Vauxhall Motors they were all issued with mobile phones. The job involved a great deal of driving and meetings with clients. Most of the calls made went straight to voicemail. However, it was company policy that they recorded a new voice message every day, and that message would start with confirming the day and date. Anyone calling would know instantly that they checked their phone and voicemail at least once a day. He also promised to return their call by the end of the working day. This often meant that he would end up leaving a message on their voicemail before eventually making contact. The important point here is that the client knew the way he handled calls and would be confident that the call would returned as promised. Returning calls from clients speedily is something appreciated by your customers.

I personally have had clients say to me, "Why is it so hard to get a hold of a DJ?" So imagine how good you will look simply by answering the phone quickly. The same applies to email. Respond as quickly as you can even if it's only to acknowledge receipt and to advise that you will give a detailed reply as soon as possible.

Always be early for appointments. In my book if you are not five minutes early you are late. There is nothing worse than sloppy punctuality. Time is the most valuable commodity there is. You can't make time but you can waste it. Wasting other people's time will not earn you any brownie points: quite the opposite. Make a point of being on time and be prepared. Keeping your meetings short, concise and on track will be greatly appreciated by others.

This also applies to your arrival at a venue for your performance. If your contract says you need an hour to set up make sure you get there with two hours to spare. Remember to allow yourself plenty of time to reach the location, keeping in mind possible traffic issues. Avoid unnecessary stress and arrive at your venue relaxed and confident. Appearing stressed and hurried will not help your image.

I will always arrive at a venue three hours before guests are due to take their seats, not that it takes me that long to set up, simply to allow for any unforeseen issues and give me time to rehearse and do my job properly as the Master of Ceremonies.

Introduce yourself to the venue management and staff. Be nice to them. Say please and thank you even when they are not being the most cooperative. People will eventually mirror your behaviour to them. It's hard to be rude to someone who is being so nice. Take time to seek out other service providers and take an interest in what they are doing for your client. Exchange business cards and check that nothing has changed unexpectedly that you were not aware of.

Complete your equipment set-up and sound check as professionally as possible. Make sure everything is tidy and safe. A good tip is to take a photograph once you have finished. It's amazing what you see in a photograph which you miss when looking with the naked eye. Move your vehicle to a safe place and ensure that you are not blocking any other cars or exits. The last thing you want is to be asked to move your van right before the bride and groom's first dance.

Once you have changed into your performance clothes and you have music running take some time to mingle with the guests. If you are not required to be in full 'DJ mode' at this time it's a nice touch to go walkabout and chat informally with the guests. This will pay big dividends during the evening when you need their input either for interaction or dancing.

If guests find you to be approachable and charming they will be encouraged to ask for music requests and may well make positive comparisons with 'lesser' DJs who they may have experienced previously. Something as simple as standing by the door greeting guest as they arrive and pointing them in the right direction will make you stand out from the average DJ.

At the end of the night take time out to say thank you to all of those present. Seek out your client who may by this time be in another part of the building. Remember to say goodbye to the venue staff and other service providers if they are still there. Investing another fifteen minutes giving positive feedback while having a cup of tea or coffee at the end of the night will confirm to others your commitment to service.

Following up after the event

This is where a lot of service providers fall down. All too often the temptation is to move on and concentrate on the next event and to neglect what happened yesterday or last week. Okay, in the case of weddings there is usually a honeymoon to be considered. The bride and groom will not appreciate you trying to contact them at this time. However, you do need a system which will enable you to seek feedback and testimonials once they have returned from their honeymoon.

If you have done your pre-event planning you will know where they are going and when they will be back. You will have already obtained their permission to follow up with them and agreed how they would like to be contacted. Personally I would not rely on one method of communication. If I were to post an evaluation form to them I would follow up with a phone call or email a couple of days later just to confirm that they had received it.

There is a popular understanding by those who do this kind of follow-up that it is best conducted by a neutral party. People tend to be more honest when they are not personally connected. It may be that they do not wish to hurt your feelings and are reluctant to tell you how they really feel about something you did. So maybe an alternative method of seeking feedback would be to employ someone else to conduct a telephone appraisal on your behalf. Negative feedback can be gold if reacted to positively.

You may wish to show your appreciation to your client by sending them a gift. This could be a bunch of flowers or a box of chocolates or maybe a bottle of wine. Anything you do which is a genuine gesture of appreciation will not only be welcomed, it will be valued! How many other DJs or service providers will have done such a thing? Probably none. We used to send a 'thank you' card.

A 'thank you' card is a very sincere gesture. Your bride and groom will no doubt be sending similar cards to their guests. It is a customary and traditional method of communicating one's thanks for attending the wedding and for any present received. A greeting card by its very nature is also designed to be kept and displayed for a while about the house or office. It is also therefore guaranteed to be shown to, and shared with, other members of the family and friends who may visit your clients. We would also try to personalise the card in order to make it a special memento of their big day. There are many ways this can be achieved, some expensive and time consuming while others are easier and equally impressive.

Send out cards

In the past I would send out a generic card with a personal message inside, then Derek introduced me to companies who specialise in producing custom greeting cards online. There are many: Yellowpostie and Moonpig, to name two. I found the quality of the cards to be very good and the reaction from those clients who received them was very encouraging. This is how we gained quality referrals and demonstrated our care and commitment to our clients.

We would obtain a good quality picture taken on the day of the wedding and using this technology created a customised card which featured them and their guests. The message would be a simple "Congratulations" or "Best wishes" from me. The card would, without exception, prompt the recipient to call us up and thank us in return for our thoughtful gesture. Imagine their pleasure upon receiving this card with a picture of their wedding day from their DJ. What do you think they will do with that card I'm betting it's the first time they have seen that done and will probably show and tell everyone?

As they say, "It's the thought that counts".

Derek uses SendOutCards: it has a neat contact manager which allows you to store all of your client's details in one place. Furthermore you can programme the system so that it will remind you of important birthdays or anniversaries. This means that you can send cards to clients automatically without having to remember when they should be sent. So now our clients not only get an anniversary card from us, they also get birthday and Christmas cards.

Why should we be doing this?

Keeping in touch with satisfied customers is the best way for them to keep you in their mind. Who knows how many opportunities they will have over a year to recommend you to people they may know? Now I know we would probably expect them to recommend us anyway, based upon what we did for them; however, human nature can be very fickle. Sometimes people need a nudge or a prompt or are reluctant to offer advice without invitation. These cards simply establish a 'relationship' with our clients, which has now progressed beyond that of service provider and client. We are now friends of the family who care to remember their special dates.

Imagine receiving a one-year anniversary card from you and just as they stopped telling everyone how good the DJ was at their wedding they receive this and it starts all over again.

One bride even told me that I was the only one out of all her vendors and even guests who sent her a card. We also used the same method to keep in touch with other service providers and venue management. We would try to customise their cards to reflect their service and we would use their images so that the card was special to them.

Once again this helped keep our company to the forefront of their minds which led to many referrals.

Understanding the power of the 'thank you' card is perhaps a little difficult at first. It took me a long time to appreciate how this worked. However, I can honestly testify to the success of using a system like this to keep in touch with your previous customers. They are your ambassadors. They will promote your service for free. In fact, using SOC increased Derek's turnover in the first year of use by over forty percent! Now I am not saying it will increase your business by that much; however, I am saying that it is well worth a try.

16] Coaching
By Jason A. Jones and Bill Herman
creators of The Entertainment Experience.
www.entertainment-expeirence.com

Everything in this book is great! and if you only implemented half of what you read in here you will have a very successful business. Many who read this book will become excited and energized by the possibility of a highly successfully multi-talent or solo talent business. Half of those who become energized will actually begin taking the steps toward making the dream a reality and the other half will talk themselves out it before even starting. Of those who act half will fail or give up.

In Australia during 2012, there were more businesses that ceased to operate than there were that started that same year. It seems pretty universal everywhere. Far more small businesses fail than succeed. And why is that?

Matt LaBlanc, author of Growing Your Business, says "this failure is not a matter of capital or losing to the competition. It's a lack of courage and creativity that leads to a lack of customers."

It takes a lot of courage to press on in your own business. And what stops us, kills our success, leads us on a path of demise is ourselves. We are always our own worst enemy when it comes to achieving something we are not quite sure we are capable of. Creativity comes in when we are willing to take new actions in order to produce new results. If people are not buying your services you begin to look at what is happening in the market place, identify what is missing in your offerings or yourself and try a new set of actions to capture new customers interest. That is not our tendency as humans. Our tendency is to learn what we need to know to attain a certain level of success that we can be comfortable with and keep taking the same actions over and over.

What will limit you?

For most of us what limits us comes from a life time of self-awareness and discovery. One highly effective way to discover, identify the source and overcome limitations is with a coach. High stakes performers have long had coaches to constantly improv their performance. Tiger Woods would not be the golfer he is had he not had years of coaching. Director/Actor Ron Howard's daughter Bryce Howard has a life coach to achieve her personal and performance goals. Steve Jobs had Brad Smith.

What does a coach do?

A coach is someone who is in complete agreement with you in terms of what you think you can achieve. A coach walks you through the a discovery process by which you learn what you really want and what really matters to you. Once that is established the path of action becomes obvious. A coach calls you forward when you get stuck and feel confused. A coach works with you to clear the confusion and give up the negative self-talk so you see your path to action and more importantly take an action. We have way more power to create than we think we do.

Coaches use a variety of tools to being out your best performance both on stage and in business.

• A coach helps you discover the most effective actions to take to reach your goals
• A coach keeps you from giving up or quitting when the goal looks too big or the work feels too hard.
• A coach demands your best performance and holds you to your promises
• A coach sees what is possible for you even when you don't
• A coach gets you back in action when you get overwhelmed or paralysed

What is great about being coached is that you decide how big a game you want to play. You could take on being the most accomplished and most famous wedding entertainer in the world. And your coach will talk to you as though you are that accomplished and famous entertainer. With you coach you will discover what actions are necessary to create that kind of fame and accomplishment. And from the day that you create you are the most famous wedding entertainer in the world you become that person. Every focused action you complete will have you achieve your goal.

Success is not elusive or magic. Success is a product of commitment and consistent action.

What types of coaches are there?

Coaching is a big unregulated field that has come from sports and the arts and has expanded into business and personal endeavours. There are lots of coaches working individual niches with many specialties. The following are the 3 main categories that can make the biggest difference for a wedding DJ.

Business coaching

Business coaches work on setting up goals and milestones to achieve your desired result and often have expertise in your field of business or business in general. Every week your business coach works to keep you focused on completing actions that are going to result in hitting your goals. Most times business coaches will not address personal issues that are affecting you and your business. The focus is on the business

Life Coaching

Life coaches take a 360 degree approach and will work with you to look at what might be in the way of having the life/success you want, achieving personal and professional goals, contentment and happiness. Your business goals may be a large part of your life coaching. Though the life coach may not know your business, they will understand how to empower you and help you develop habits that enhance your performance in every area of life.

Performance Coaching

In the context of the DJ business, performance speaks to the many forms of performance art that a wedding DJ can take. Making announcements and calling out the bouquet toss is not a service performed by a technician. It's a stage performance and a performance coach can identify ways to improve your connection to the audience, polish your presentation and help you find authenticity in your act. The performance coach should have experience in your field and various other forms of stage performance like public speaking, acting and/or directing.

Workshops in comedy, acting, speaking, improvisation or wedding DJ industry specific workshops (like Mark Ferrell's MC workshop and Love Story Workshop and the Entertainment Experience Workshops) can all dramatically improve your stage performance and value to clients. This can lead to greater confidence, higher fees and greater satisfaction in your performance.

More importantly, training results in the discovery of what makes you and your performance unique and valuable. You know the question, "What is your unique selling proposition?" In the art of the wedding entertainer what is unique is you. Your style, your like-ability, how fun you are. The more you train the more you discover what it is that you bring to the party that sets you a part from everyone and makes you more valuable.

Working on an ongoing basis with a performance coach can accelerate the advancement of your skill, poise, and confidence with velocity.

How do I find a Coach?

There are certifications like the International Coaches Federation to help ensure those who call themselves coaches have trained to deliver coaching. And though the certification has merit there are many different trainings and experiences that can develop a successful coach.

So first look to your industry. Are there any high performers in your market using coaches and who are they? Look to coaches with experience in the entertainment business. Even though it's not necessary to know your business niche to be an effective coach, having a coach who knows the unique challenges and opportunities in your business can be a plus.

Once you have settled on a couple candidates to be your coach it's time to interview them. You will want to know what qualifies them to coach, their coaching method and get three references.

In the interview, have them explain how you will produce results with their coaching, how they like to work and how they handle over coming limitations that are inevitable with big goals. Then call the references and ask them about the results they have produced during coaching. Ask them what has been the most effective about the coaching. Between due diligence and your intuition about the individual you interviewed you will know who is the right coach for you.

Fear of failure used to stop me faster than anything before I started working with a coach. I would see the possibility of being a nationally syndicated talk show host, or an international speaker/trainer. And then I would run a huge list of scenarios in my imagination to see all the pit-falls and ways I could fail. It didn't take very long before I was dropping that idea and moving on to the next that was smaller and more feasible (I would tell myself).

My coach asked to me to consider that when things don't work out and doors close, that I should let that inform me of what to do next rather than be a barometer on whether I was succeeding for failing. He asked me to consider that success is staying in action. If the actions didn't produce the results I was looking for that I embrace new actions.

It was that little insight that became a breakthrough in my performance and has propelled me forward ever since. I don't spend much time thinking about whether I'm failing or succeeding now. Every challenge, every "no", every disagreement with my grand plan for my life just informs me of what there is to do next to fulfil it. Spending time and energy being upset over how I think a situation "should go" only wastes energy and I don't like being upset.

It's not that "being upset" doesn't happen or that I don't get scared, doubt myself or worry. I do all of those things. What is different is that with practice I can recognize my own limiting patterns that show up and continue taking actions toward my goal. I am going to feel lots of things and do my share of negative self-talk during my life. Those feelings and thoughts will come and go.

Only my actions will make my dreams a reality.

17] THE FUTURE

If I had a crystal ball, or better still a magic wand, what sort of mobile wedding DJ industry would I like to see in the future? What would I hope had changed and how would that change have been achieved? Allow me if you will to indulge my fantasy; you never know, my dreams may come true … one day!

In these times of economic pressure I guess it is safe to assume that money will be harder to come by and that competition will be fiercer than ever before. Further development of compact sound and lighting systems will mean that more and more wannabe DJs will be on the street looking to earn a dollar or two. Nothing new so far, this situation exists today as it has done for the last ten years or more.

Oversupply in a marketplace will always drive prices down. That is why it is so important for you as a mobile DJ to stand out from the crowd as a truly unique talent. Talent is something which is valued. If you admire and respect someone for their talent you acknowledge that person's gift. I can't read music or sing in tune. I can't play an instrument or speak a foreign language. Therefore I stand in awe of a performer who can take to a stage and entertain an audience.

I would hope, in the future, to see disc jockeys marketing themselves for their talent. Yet how do we define talent when it comes to what we do? How do we get our clients to understand that being a mobile DJ is not easy, that not everyone can do it, especially to a high standard? How do we raise the bar so that in the future it is clear and obvious who the professional wedding specialist entertainers are?

Certification or accreditation

Maybe there will be an official accreditation of mobile disc jockeys. In the future disc jockeys may have to pass an examination before they are allowed to perform. There could be a series of levels of professionalism or service standards. The levels could be based upon how long the DJ has been in business or the number of weddings he has performed at, or maybe on testimonials obtained by the governing body.

This has been suggested before but while it sounds good in theory the practicalities are strewn with anomalies. Who would sit in judgement? How would it be administered and, more importantly, policed? It would probably have to be organised by a nationally recognised trade association and thereby stands the first hurdle because none exists. How much would such a certification scheme cost and, more importantly, how much would DJs be prepared to pay each year to maintain their accreditation?

Licensing

There is another route whereby something similar may be achieved in the not-too-distant future. Currently local authorities are responsible for licensing premises which provide alcohol and entertainment to the general public. So why shouldn't they be encouraged to take on the administration of a licensing scheme for entertainers? Okay, it would only cover the bare minimum of criteria such as public liability, electrical safety and possibly tax code and national insurance declaration. However, these basic standards would drive a huge percentage of 'cowboys' out of the industry. Musicians, singers and the numerous services provided by event management companies would also be required to be licensed.

Local authorities are strapped for cash and will be looking to increase income from new sources. They already have the mechanism in place. They already offer a similar licensing service for taxi drivers and security guards. Imagine being able to walk into a venue wearing your badge or being able to 'stop' an unlicensed DJ who is stealing your livelihood. The implications of such a scheme would, I believe, be far reaching.

Less wannabe disc jockeys together with a national requirement for a licence would help realign the pricing issue. Yes, it would initially increase the cost of doing business but this cost would be passed on to customers. There would be less competition and market forces would work in our favour. The more I think about such a scheme the more possibilities come to mind.

If there was a local register of licensed mobile disc jockeys the general public would be able to find them listed, in one place, for the first time ever. How cool would that be? It would mean that DJs would not need necessarily to spend as much as they do on marketing. Alternatively their marketing would be enhanced by the inclusion of their licensing details.

Of course, there would be a down side to such a scheme. Failure to comply, at least once a year, would result in an expired licence. An expired licence would mean inability to work and loss of income. If the scheme proved profitable to local authorities you can guarantee the cost of licensing will increase year on year. However, I do not see these issues as a problem; on the contrary, I see them as regulations to be complied with at my peril.

I see them as a test of my business acumen. I would expect others to feel the same way.

Competition will, I predict, still be rife. However, I would hope that the ridiculously low amounts earned would have disappeared. In the future mobile DJs will, I hope, have learned their lesson. The starting price for the services of a mobile DJ should at least be above the alternative of hiring the equipment, delivery and collection, set-up and strip-down, and the hourly rate of pay for an audio / video technician.

Admittedly my crystal ball is a little cloudy and in need of good polish. If my ideas on licensing are little more than a pipe dream maybe there is something which could be achieved by the industry as it stands today.

Education is the key

There has always been a lot of talk about education but up until recently there has been very little action in providing content. Education, like marketing, needs to be targeted. Who needs educating and who will be the teachers? What subjects need to be taught and where will the pupils come from? As usual the issues of cost and who will pay for providing the education will be the cornerstone on which training is provided.

Training mobile disc jockeys

There are some that would argue that you can't train a mobile DJ. Many believe that self-taught is the only way, or the traditional way. Some say that the talent or skill is intuitive. You either have a natural aptitude or you don't. Ego raises its head and takes over from reason. Many believe they have nothing to learn and that they know all they need to know about being a mobile disc jockey. Hopefully in the future these opinions will have changed, but I doubt it.

There are places where those who seek training can go. Formal training is offered by a small number of companies and even fewer local authorities and charitable organisations. Most training schemes are designed for music production and performance. The target market is usually, but not exclusively, for club and radio disc jockeys.

A quick Google search will reveal what may be available in your area.

Some multi-operator DJ companies are looking to recruit people from other 'regular' employment and train them as disc jockeys.

I remember one such company telling me that they preferred teachers or bar staff because they had a natural ability to communicate with others. Recruiting such staff greatly reduces the 'ego' challenge and enables the trainers to concentrate on ability.

DJ associations do their best, especially those who support live events or which hold regular meetings. However, they are usually not in a position to offer specific one-on-one training. The best these organisations can hope for is to provide some form of mentoring or distance learning on ad-hoc topics.

Who knows what the future may bring? Probably most disc jockeys will still be self-taught or will have learnt from a single DJ who they know. Hopefully standards will have risen and he or she will be more knowledgeable than their predecessors. There may be more training available and they may be more receptive to it. Better still, they may well be seeking out training opportunities and encouraging their trade representatives to provide more.

Let's leave training to one side and take a look at what could be done by way of general education.

The public:

While we as mobile disc jockeys know what it is we do as a service provider it is probably fair to say that the general public have very little knowledge on the subject. Stereotypical images can be very powerful and extremely misleading. This is even more of a concern for wedding specialists.

Disc jockeys currently have no nationally recognised governing body but they do have a number of organisations previously mentioned here who claim to represent the industry. So far they have directed most of their time and limited resources to supporting their members within the confinement of equipment and performance. Maybe, in the future, they should direct their attention to seeking out and educating our potential clients.

Live interactive advice:

However, what associations, forums and individuals can do is promote the services provided by its collective membership or company. Therefore I would like to see a time when advertisements were placed in bridal magazines featuring the benefits of choosing a member over a non-member.

Articles written by leading members should offer advice about hiring a mobile disc jockey. Brides should be encouraged to visit a 'client area' of websites where they can ask questions and receive impartial advice. Maybe a live chat room service could be provided for instant communication.

There is a demand on television for dedicated wedding-focused reality programming but we are yet to see anything which features or is sponsored by a DJ organisation. The possibilities are endless. I would love to see an internet radio station hosted by wedding DJs playing a variety of music while taking calls or texts from brides and maybe connecting them with service providers in their area.

None of the above will be easy to achieve. Money and resources will need to be found and allocated. However, I believe that membership will increase dramatically once disc jockeys see that the message is getting through. Imagine the day when the first question asked by a client is not "How much?" but "Are you a member of XXXX?" or better still "I understand you are the best wedding DJ in the area, are you available for our wedding?"

Finally, may I thank you for reading this book, especially those who paid for a copy. May I wish you well in all that you attempt and success as a specialist wedding disc jockey.

Hopefully you will have found some 'nuggets' within these pages which you can use to help grow your business or improve your marketing. If you would like to contact me feel free to email at

john@weddingdjworkshops.com.au

And remember:

"It's not what you do, it's how you do it" which gets results.

18] TIPS FROM OTHER DJs

Mobile DJs are almost without exception self-taught. In this section of the book I have invited a few fellow talented colleagues from Australia and around the world to share their stories. They have all taken different paths yet have arrived at the same destination. It's also no coincidence that they have not undertaken their journey alone. Along the way they have sought support and advice and have been open to new ideas and constructive criticism. Now they want to share some of what they have learnt in the hope that it helps you on your journey.

Steve Bowen
Chairperson, DJ Alliance Australasia
Managing Director, Bowens Entertainment
www.bowensentertainment.com.au

Performance – "What else do you do other than play music?"

Steve Bowen has been an MC/DJ Entertainer since 1984 in Albury/Wodonga initially working for others until he started his own company - Bowens Entertainment in 1989. Steve now MC's & DJ's at weddings and events all over Australia & internationally because of his 'unique' DJ Entertainer style and he still continues to live in the Albury/Wodonga region.

Here's some of Steve Bowen's story:

It was sometime back in the mid 1990's that I had a 'Light bulb' moment (for me anyway). I went to see the Four Kinsmen perform when they came through town and I was amazed at not only the variety of entertainment at their show but also at how engaged the audience of 500 people were, with ages ranging from as young as 8 years old to 80 years young. They performed a variety of entertainment including life sized puppets, magic, comedy, skits, dance, singing, music, acrobatics and heaps of different props, it was fantastic!

It was after the Four Kinsmen Show that I started to ask myself "what else can I do with my performance other than just playing music"? That's when I realised there was a whole world of different things I could do and consider to introduce to my events. So I made a list of things I could do for a wedding such as MC, singing (not a great option for me lol), interaction with guests, magic, games, humour, photos, requests, juggling, fireworks and even origami with napkins etc. Not that I did all of these things but I wanted to see what the possibilities were to enhance the experience for the client.

This really made me think about how I could be different from every other DJ out there and how I could create my own unique style. I always had a meeting with my clients before their wedding to discuss their music but it never occurred to me to ask any more about them until after my little 'light bulb' moment. I started to find out a little more about their likes and dislikes and I started to ask this question that changed my business and performance forever…..

"What is the most important thing I can do for you at your wedding"?

Then I started to get some incredible answers from my couples that had nothing to do with the music I was to play. This really helped me understand that there were other things to focus on that were more important to the clients as well as good music (which I thought was the only import thing I had to consider previously).

This opened up a whole new world to my events especially weddings as well as my feedback from clients. I introduced MCing into my events, don't get me wrong, I always thought I MCéd fairly well before but I was really only making general announcements, now I really MC with more confidence and a lot more background knowledge about my clients because I practiced, practiced and practiced every chance I got.

This was just one adjustment I had introduced to my performance that made a huge impact with my weddings. So I gradually introduced more and more new items (new for me) into every event I performed and I thought I'd share just some of them so you can consider what else you can do other than just playing music (like most DJ's) to create your own unique style.

Prior to wedding
• Preparation is king – meet with your wedding couple on a number of occasions (at least three times where possible) to support them with the planning process and to foster creative ideas that suit their style and personalities.
• Make contact with the bride and groom's parents well before the wedding day to introduce yourself and ask if they have any special requirements (the parents are usually blown away and are very appreciative to be thought of)
• Contact the venue and meet with the wedding co-ordinator

(where possible) to view the set-up area, load in/out requirements, noise restrictions (if any), parking availability, timeline and anything else you need to know.
• Make contact with other vendors associated with the day eg. Photographer, Florist, Celebrant, Videographer, wedding decorator and anyone else you want to connect with.
• Consider going to the wedding rehearsal, if you've never done this before, try it out and see what an impact it has on the success of the wedding. Not only is it great to see the ceremony format it gives you a chance to meet the wedding party and other people integral to their wedding day so on the actual wedding day you know a few people and they know you.

Wedding day

• Set up nice and early so you have plenty of time for any challenges.
• Go to the ceremony (where possible) and experience all that happens. Support them with their music if possible take a few candid photos.
• Be the first to the reception – then you are able to control the room much easier. Welcome guests into reception or pre-dinner area and introduce yourself to guests with a smile. Show them to their seats, where the gift table is located, get them to sign the signature book and generally make them feel welcome (do this even if you're not MC)
• If you are the MC – Open with a welcoming smile and let guests know the order of proceedings make people feel welcome and comfortable. Consider starting or ending your opening address with an ice breaker.
• Introduce the wedding party into the room with the atmosphere to reflect the bride and groom's style (which you would have planned during your prior meetings)
• Introduce the parents and even grandparents to the guests (especially if the parents have been involved with the wedding planning)
• Give out music request forms to guests to get them involved with the atmosphere (if ok'd by bride and groom in prior meetings)
• Take a few candid photos and display them (and the photos you took at the ceremony) on a TV screen or projector.
• Involve guests and wedding party with some fun activities, quiz's, competitions or games.
• Fun dances, dance-offs, conga lines, circular dances or other nationality dances or even make up some of your own (that everyone can do).
• Switch the focus – make them feel involved and part of the entertainment.
• Interaction with guests – how much is too little or too much? What are some things you could do that are subtle and yet create atmosphere in the room.

- Do you use any props to enhance a mood or activity?
- Creating special moments like bridal dance, father/daughter dance, mother/son dance, parent dance, ribbon dance, dollar dance etc.
- Keep things F-U-N Flowing-Unique-Nice.
- Get out from behind your console! You are not a jukebox… are you?
- Smile, Smile & Smile some more, lead by example - if you're not having a good time, why should everyone else?

After Wedding

- Always ask for feedback.
- Contact wedding couple after honeymoon to thank them for choosing you.
- Email feedback form or if posting feedback form send with reply paid envelope to ensure its return.
- Email or Send copy of candid photos taken on day.

Once again these are just 'some' examples of what you can do for a wedding (and there are plenty more) that doesn't involve playing music but I don't under estimate how important it is to know your music and how crucial it is to the success of an event as well.

Obviously some things will work for some clients and not be appropriate for other clients. It's up to you to work out what suits you, your style and your individual client's requirements because every event is always different.

So I'll ask you one more time…

"What else do you do other than play music?"

Best wishes with evolving into a DJ Entertainer or as I like to call it an 'EJ'.

Mark Wall – INFINITY ENTERTAINMENT
www.infinityentertainment.com.au

Mark is the owner and manager of Infinity Entertainment and Infinity Audio Visual. His extensive business background is supported by his diploma and bachelor degree in graphic design / multimedia and his roles in marketing and business development for corporate and government bodies.

Mark's passion is in entertainment and business development; his business is a standout in the entertainment industry where he aims to exceed client expectations.

It's a great honour to be asked to contribute to a book that is designed specifically for the entertainment industry and mobile disco operators. Over the years I have found that our industry isn't always treated seriously and I honestly believe this image can be changed.

When John Beck approached key figures in the industry I asked myself, what would I discuss? What has helped me shape my business and what has set me apart from the endless number of competitors in the industry?

The answer, for me, is simple but daunting. And to others they would consider it a crazy concept.

In simple terms I learnt I had to say "No".

It seems a rather odd solution but one of the lessons I learnt a very long time ago is that my time, my business, my family and our commitment to our clients is worth something. Putting a value on our service set a precedent for how my business would grow.

Saying no to specific types of work and structuring my business around what we are good at has helped shape the way I work today and in turn how I have grown the company to the stage we are at today.

Now this is where everyone within the industry shakes their head and says something along the lines of, "Here we go again … yet another 'getting what you're worth' discussion." But hear me out. It's a view that has worked for me, and like anything it has limits but has certainly helped with the success of my business.

Like most people I started in the entertainment industry through a friend or family member. In this instance I started working for my brother Gary who operated Infinity Entertainment in the Shepparton area, Central Victoria. He was winding down his involvement within the industry as a growing family and other work commitments took priority. Naturally, however, the calls kept coming.

As Gary had stepped back, I had the opportunity to make some extra cash and inevitably found myself working for other companies eager to get another DJ on board. Of course, they paid very little, their approach was rather questionable and the quality of equipment, service and passion were lacking at best. I quickly said to myself, is this what I would do if I was running a similar business?

Luckily enough I already had a good grounding for what to expect with a mobile DJ business so in 2005 I re-registered Infinity Entertainment and set out to provide high-end mobile discos to a flooded market. What was I thinking …

The first year was slow; I was studying graphic design / multimedia and was only offering my services to the few friends and family members that required it. As time went on more and more bookings came in the door and I soon found myself in the situation where I was outlaying a considerable amount of money for equipment and training yet I was getting no return on investment. Friends would ask, can you do my birthday, and inevitably, I would say "Yes …"

The problem was, every time I said "Yes …" the bank balance remained in the negative. I spent my hours working for free, albeit for friends, and quickly discovered I needed to treat the business as a business if I was going to make a success through the industry.

So … I said "No". Suddenly my Saturday nights weren't spent with friends but rather with clients who became friends.

Now you start to see a trend:

-Sorry I cannot afford to take on a job for $200, I will lose money.
-No, sorry, I can't provide free up-lighting in this situation.
-No, you can't borrow my speakers for your band, they are, however, available for hire.

With this in mind it's important that every time I say no to something it is strategic. Firstly I may have another goal in mind or I simply may not be in a position to say yes. By being honest to yourself and your business you start to attract the customers you need to stay in business.

So this is where I head off track for a paragraph or two. By changing my view on who I said yes and no to I started to attract customers who valued what I had to offer. Suddenly I wasn't just some DJ, I was Mark, the Master of Ceremonies or Mark from Infinity Entertainment. The name started to change and so did the clientele.

A perfect example of this was at a thirtieth birthday when I was just starting out. I quoted $300 and got the job, no questions asked. I put in all of the legwork, I spent countless hours preparing and ensuring I had everything perfect. Towards the end of the evening as a few more drinks disappeared from the bar, the guests became unbearable. They quite simply didn't value me, the effort I had put in or the passion I had. The night was horrible.

Fast forward ten years and the only thing that has changed is the price, a few processes and maybe some gear. But the effect is astounding. We are treated with respect, we are valued and we are a part of something very special.

Now, it's important to note, we put a lot of energy and effort into every event and yes, there are a million variations to this rule ... but the general idea is clear.

On the positive side to this example is that now I can choose to spend time at home, spend time training, spend time networking or simply DJ a friend's wedding because I am now in a position to do so ...

I have also been able to contribute back to the industry through pieces like this or through the DJ Alliance of Australia and local networking groups.

Thomas Ormond
Formerly known as Soundclash Entertainment.
And producer on SBS Radio.
www.thomasormond.com.au

Let us stop for a moment and imagine a scenario here;

A 29 year old club DJ, walking out of Australia's Melbourne Airport for the first time in his life, after a 24 hour flight from Malta. He is still thinking of what he left behind in his homeland and with no idea of what awaits him in this new adventure.

His beautiful wife wanted to move back to Australia, where she was born and grew up, where the rest of her family lived. He was up for the new challenge, even though all he knew about this country and its people was from what he had seen on Skippy the bush kangaroo. For all the hard work in the previous ten years or so to try and become a full time club DJ, he was reaping the rewards in the last two. Finally he was earning money from doing what he loved best, playing music in a nightclub environment and drinking beer in sunny Malta but as soon as he stepped on that plane, he had to leave his dream behind.

That 29 year old club DJ was me, I am now 39 years old, an Australian citizen and I call Australia home. I am Thomas Ormond, owner and manager of Thomas Ormond Events.

Before I continue, I am just going to let you know that I was honoured to have been asked by John Beck to give some tips on this book but I am just going to share my story with you as I feel that you may get more from it than if I give you a tip or two, not to mention the awesome work already done on this project by John, Derek and the other contributors.

This is my story.

The difficulties that every immigrant who moves to Australia will face is the fact that this nation, because of its diversity, is so different from any other nation that sometimes even if you are an expert in one field or another, what you specialised in, in another country, might not be relevant here. That also seemed to be an issue in my situation. Apart from not being able to communicate well in English with others because of the fact that Australian English sounded very different from the European and American English that I am used to, and the fact that English is not my first language, I also had difficulties communicating with Maltese-Australians as the Maltese language in Malta is spoken at a faster pace and only a few people could really understand me properly. At the start I was really getting frustrated by all this as all I wanted to do was to get back behind the decks and start entertaining people, after all that is what I was good at.

I started to look for some DJ work on online forums and I managed to get a few contacts, where I had the opportunity to play in a few bars and clubs but unlike Malta at the time, most club DJs in Australia, also act as promoters and they get paid depending on how many people they have on the guest list. That might work if you are a single 18 year old with a lot of friends from high school or if you are a big name DJ but for a married man who only just arrived in the country, the only friends I could think of where on the other side of the planet.

My father-in-law suggested that I should get involved more in the Maltese community in Victoria and that I should try and DJ at some of the events organised by the Maltese. I told him I did not want to do that, my mobile DJing days were long gone. He managed to persuade me into going to a few events with him to see what it's all about. I designed and printed some business cards and on the road we went, me and my new unofficial manager, every dinner dance and social night, we were there, me and him and before I even knew it, the bookings started coming in. It was here when I realised this might work and I went and bought all the gear I thought I needed and registered a business. I still was not a hundred percent happy as this was not really what I wanted to do but in my life I learnt that when a door opens, you either grab the opportunity to walk in or close it and miss that opportunity.

I needed to update my music library heavily as most of my music collection consisted mainly of house music and now I found myself playing the party classics and the oldies. In the process I started to explore various genres and I enjoyed listening to other music rather than just what I was used too. All of a sudden I was not just focusing on one style of music or one type of audience but I opened a few other opportunity doors. It was here when I started watching DJ related YouTube videos and came across John Beck's channel.

The first time I met John was when a young lady told me that she saw me DJing at a dinner dance and she wanted me to DJ at her wedding but I was already booked. I did not even know what networking was back then and I only knew one other DJ but I wanted to help her by referring someone who I believed that can do a great job at her big day.

I thought of John and his videos, looked up his number and gave him a call and from then on I realised that there was more to DJing than what I knew.

John Beck wanted to see DJs get involved in networking so when he asked for help, I decided that one way I could offer assistance was by creating a Facebook Group, which back then I named The Revolution DJ Group as the aim was to change the perception of how DJs were looked at and how we as an industry looked at ourselves. We organised a networking meeting with the help of a few other DJs which attracted about 30 people who all agreed that our industry needed an industry body. After the meeting we decided that the 'DJ revolution' was done and now it was time for DJs to start evolving, The group name was changed to The EVO and it is still running to this day with over a 100 DJs sharing their knowledge and networking. In our second networking meeting Peter De Wever was present and he informed us that together with James Cottingham, he had already started what we now know as the DJAA and as a group The EVO decided that rather than trying to come up with something different, those who were looking to work on some form of body within the industry, should become part of the DJAA.

My business was going great with most of my bookings coming from the Maltese Community but I was also getting referrals and work from other DJs from the group and vice-versa. At this time, thanks to networking sessions like these, we were learning more about each other and if we needed to refer someone to a potential client, we could recommend the right person. Something that most of the group members are still doing to this day.

We also started to see a lot of DJ, MC & Business workshops, by local and foreign DJs, MCs and other speakers which saw a number of DJs step up their game and were able to charge a lot more for their services. Although there were times where the industry was split over the idea of whether or not one should raise his or her prices so that they can earn a living, take part and spend thousands of dollars in training workshops and the need of an industry body, today we can say that thanks to those who did not give up, our industry is at a better place than where it was 5, 10 or 15 years ago.

It has not been an easy ride but I am today enjoying being a full time Mobile DJ business owner. Unlike most of the other leaders in the industry, my business is not run primarily on weddings. Most of my bookings come from those Maltese community clubs which are still happy with my services after all these years, even though my prices have gone up drastically. These are the same events that I did not want to do ten years ago but the relationships and friendships that I have developed with the committees within these clubs and their members, is something that not many are lucky to experience when running a business and especially when it involves being of service to a community that you are part of. My services to the Maltese community do not stop there either. Thanks to all the networking, friendships I developed through the years in our industry and all the workshops I attended, I am also a broadcasting journalist and producer for the Maltese program on one of the main national radio stations in Australia. This gives me a wonderful opportunity to share Malta with Australians and Australia with the Maltese people, something I am really proud of.

I am where I am today because even at this age, I still listen to those who try and help me. Those who tried to put me down, and yes there has been a few, are no longer part of my life. I am at an age that when I need help, I do not want to be scared to ask for it. That is why I surround myself with people who wish me all the best, those who want me to succeed, those who guide me when I need to be guided, those who offer me their helping hand to help me get outside the box rather than want to see me stay inside it, those who see me as a friend rather than their competition, those who look up to me even though they know I look up to them.

I am where I am because you gave me some of your precious time to read all this to get inspired and I want to give you a reason to do so and even try and give you something back. I am no different from you, no better, no worse. I, like many others, suffer from glossphobia - fear of public speaking - and I choose to challenge myself to speak in front of people rather than walk away from my fear. I know that if I want to do this for the rest of my life, I have got to be ready to take the whole package that comes with it. I was never a businessman, web designer, event co-ordinator or any other job title that you require to run a successful DJ business and I was never a journalist either. I could hardly communicate with the people of this beautiful country, when I walked out of the Melbourne Airport ten years ago but somehow I find myself contributing to this excellent book. If I can do it, so can you.

Finally start looking at what's really important in your life, respect your fellow DJs and learn the meaning of the word LOVE!!! Love yourself, love your friends and those around you, love what you got and love what you do. That is all you need to be happy and successful. Everything else is just a bonus!

Peter de Wever AKA DJ PeterD Entertainment Plus
www.djpeterd.com.au

DJ PeterD Entertainment Plus was formed in 2008 in Victoria, Australia after working in the industry since 1978 when I started as a jock playing music at an ice skating rink and doing my first engagement party at 18, and it just went up from there. I tried the working-for-myself thing but found it easier to work for other multi-ops until I left Perth, Western Australia in 2006.

I moved to New Zealand where I did a couple of events in my two years there but when I moved to Victoria in 2008 it was decided to go it alone!!! I have since won awards and runners-up in the DJ and MC categories with the Australian Bridal awards in 2011, 2012, 2013 and 2014.

The tips I would give to anyone looking at making this their chosen profession is:

Remember where you started and remember how you looked in the day!!

Do not judge others in the industry based on your level of expertise.

Be open to ideas old and new and be prepared to change.

Just because someone charges less or more does not mean they are worse or better than you.

Set your fee at a level that you are happy with, keeping in mind that this will also reflect on the general view of the industry so make it an amount that is a liveable income.

Work with others and get ideas from others but do NOT copy what others have made their own.

There is only one of you so sell that person and not what others portray.

My personal opinion is that if the client is wearing a tux, don't wear one; always dress up, but dress down from the client.

Last and most important make the event about the client, NOT YOU; many clients are scared that the entertainment will take the limelight so let them know that it is about them.

Marketing tips:

Work out what market you would like to work in or target before you start throwing money into the pit. By all means check out what your competitors are doing for marketing but do your own style to attract your style of client.

Social and online marketing seem to be the most successful and some sites will work better for some people so sometimes you will have to do a hit and miss.

Make sure you work on your own website and make it simple and clear and easy to navigate.

One of my personal favourites is wedding expos and fairs so that potential clients can meet you, so it will help lock in bookings on a basis that they liked you and your personality.

I hope these tips help you in the move to build your dream business.

Alan Marshall
www.celebrations-mobile-disco.co.uk

Based in Andover Hampshire we provide entertainment all over the south of England Celebrations Discotheques is a mobile disco business specialising in Weddings and owned by Alan Marshall, a full time Master of Ceremonies and Wedding DJ with over 25 years' experience.

It all began back in 2008 at BPM DJ show, which back then was held at Donington Park. While visiting the show with my wife Anna Marie we sat in on a seminar by an American author, DJ and motivational speaker called Ken Day. His presentation was on the 'Soft Sell' and, in a nutshell, it was about specializing in one particular type of party, for Ken that was Weddings. While listening to Ken's talk a light went on and Anna Marie and I both had a "eureka "moment!

I loved doing weddings, but to become a specialist and not a jack of all trades seemed a large risk, surely if I covered all types of bookings I would be more bookable. On the other hand I knew if you do what you have always done you get what you have always got, and that was not working for me; after 27 years in the business, I still wasn't making enough to go full time. In fact, as a DJ back in 2008 I had an old tired website that was doing little, if not nothing, for me and I wasn't doing any social networking or visiting any forums. This was all to change.

I introduced a new website, business cards and brochure all aimed squarely at the Wedding Market. I also became hungry for information and education. After purchasing pretty much every book I could from the Pro Mobile book store, I then expanded my search further afield. While reading an article on a forum posted by Richard Mills, a DJ from Wellington in New Zealand, I discovered a collection of podcasts on iTunes from Disc Jockey America call 'DJA Radio', which changed my whole world. The 30 minute radio style podcasts presented by American mobile DJs contained a vast array of information on running a successful DJ business. It was like they were giving away the keys to the castle! I was blown away, as my experience of talking with DJs in the UK was a combination of 'bull' and 'mines bigger than yours' mentality. I felt that those DJs in the UK, with anything that made them special, closely guarded their secrets; however these guys in the US were full of free advice and tips.

While I was listening to DJA Radio I heard Mark Ferrell, owner of DJA, mention some two day workshops on 'The Love Story' and 'Master of Ceremonies'. After purchasing his 'Worth' CDs (now available via markferrell. com) I decided to take a massive leap of faith and sign up for the next workshop in February 2010 in Las Vegas which was planned to coincide with the MobileBeat DJ show. What I did not know at this point was that just a few months prior to my Las Vegas trip I found out that my daytime employer was to make me redundant. However with what I had been listening to on DJA Radio (sadly no longer available) and the support from my family and my new friends in the wider DJ community I knew that I could make a success of my DJ business.

Prior to traveling out to the States I contacted Derek Pengelly, through an online forum in the UK for advice on traveling to Las Vegas. Derek, with his wife Carol, had attended MobileBeat many times and had also attended a MarBecca workshop. He was able to provide some introductions, which made my first trip even more valuable as suddenly I was being introduced to DJs considered to be in the top 5 percent of talent in the States. Derek and Carol are now good family friends and I sincerely value their support.

The message was simple ...

Don't listen to DJs who earn less than you and say 'you can't', listen to DJs who earn more than you and say 'you can'.

What I experienced on the workshop was beyond my expectations and lit a fire within me; I now knew that I needed to do all I could to become a better performer, after all, this was now going to be my full-time job! I realized that my future is as a full-time Wedding DJ.

In 2011 I returned to Vegas to attend two new workshops and also booked a personal consultation (a whole day of one-on-one critique with Mark Ferrell, which involved looking together at a video of one of my shows and dissecting it minute by minute.

So what have I learnt? I have begun to understand that the value clients place on the benefits of a good service is reflective in the price they will pay, which has nothing to do with competition.

Also that my future is in working on my performance skills through workshops, public speaking clubs, trying to become a more rounded performer and understanding how networking with positive thinking people can help me to grow my business.

I have now attended five MarBecca workshops & along the way made some really good friends & made countless positive contacts within the industry here in the UK & around the world.

If I could sum it up in one sentence, in the words of my mentor, coach & friend Mark Ferrell "always put the client first"

Paul Arnett
www.mybigdaydj.co.uk

Paul Arnett is a former chairman of the National Association of Disc Jockeys in the UK. He has been performing for over twenty years for functions and weddings across England

I started DJing back in 1985 when I was just 15 years old and was initially intrigued by the equipment, but then fell in love with the music and the effect it could have over people. Over the next few years my range of equipment changed and evolved from home made light screens to what seemed like a multitude of pin spots, mushroom lights and the first moonflowers, with my show growing to a massive size. The gigs came in thick and fast and the extra money came in handy. Back in those days I'd work anywhere, cramming my Fiat Panda full of gear and dashing about Yorkshire eager to get those £100 gigs under my belt.

After ten years of doing this I was realising that maybe I wasn't getting what I worth. The gigs I was fighting over tended to be in quite dodgy venues, and the crowds attending probably weren't the best either, and I came to the conclusion that I wasn't prepared to put up with the hours, level of abuse, and level of pay. I had to make a decision, to shut up and put up, give it all up or radically change the way I worked.

I started chatting with a fellow DJ, Richard Mills, who had made this decision, even though he was thousands of miles away across the world. Richard advised me to look objectively at what I did. He showed me that the service was more important than the equipment and how to market myself better to get better clients, better venues and more importantly, better pay.

I re launched my DJ services squarely at the wedding market. I embraced a new way of working where customer service was king, the preparation for the gig being just as important as my performance on the night and over the next few years reaped the benefits. The gear got smaller and the job satisfaction increased as my new found way of working helped me to progress my business to where it is today.

The main thing I would attribute this to is talking to other DJs, not seeing them as competition, but as mentors and tutors helping each other so that everyone benefits.

With my involvement with NADJ and in recent months my appointment as chairman, I've made this principle one of the main concepts, that DJs will only raise their game and also the profile of the industry by talking to one another and being open to new ideas of working.

ACKNOWLEDGEMENTS

Please support these fine ambassadors for our industry and invest in their products should you have the opportunity.

Mark and Rebecca Ferrell –
Creator of the audio presentation 'Getting what you're worth', and host of DJ workshops using The MarBecca Method: www.markferrell.com

Peter Merry –
Author of The Best Wedding Reception Ever and The Six Pillars of Wedding Marketing: www.merryweddings.com

Bill Herman and Jason A. Jones –
Creators of 'The Entertainment Experience':
www.entertainment-experience.com

Randy Bartlett –
Creator of the DVD series The One Percent Solution:
http://www.dj1percentsolution.com/ and www.premierentertainment.biz

Jim Cerone –
Creator of 'The Perfect Host': www.jimcerone.com

Scott Faver –
Otherwise known as 'The Games Master': www.thepartyfavers.com

Bob Popyk –
Author of Increase Your Mobile DJ Business by 30% Starting Next Month:
http://www.promobile.org.uk/bookstore.php

Ken Day –
Co-Author of The Master Wedding MC: www.promobile.org.uk

Tom Haibeck –
Author of The Wedding MC and Wedding Toasts Made Easy available from Amazon.

Larry Williams –
Author of Mind Your Own Business: www.prodjpublishing.com

Andy [Cubby] Powell –
Author of Guerilla Marketing Companion for DJs: www.promobile.org.uk

Michael Buonaccorso –
Author of A Different Spin and Mobile Beat Show Producer:
http://www.mobilebeat.com/mobile-beat-bookstore/a-different-spin-by-michael-buonaccorso/

Robert Linquist –
Co-founder of Mobile Beat magazine

Ryan Berger –
Current owner of Mobile Beat magazine
Co-author of Turning music into Gold: www.mobilebeat.com

Ron Michaels –
http://www.ronmichaelsweddings.com/

Ed Frank –
Independent DJ and owner of Sound Entertainment:
http://www.soundentdjs.com/

Mark Walsh –
Producer of the world's biggest DJ show, BPM:
http://www.visitbpm.co.uk/

Eddie Small –
Editor and owner of Pro Mobile Magazine: http://www.promobile.org.uk/

Alan Marshall –
Independent DJ / MC: http://www.celebrations-mobile-disco.co.uk

Brian Mole –
Independent DJ / MC: http://www.facebook.com/weddingdjbrianmole

Paul Arnett –
Independent DJ / MC and chairman of the NADJ: www.nadj.org.uk
http://www.mybigdaydj.co.uk/

Richard Mills –
Independent DJ / MC: http://www.disco.co.nz/

APPENDICES

Booking form

This is a copy of the form I use to confirm a booking. It is specific to weddings and me, a guarantee that I personally will be the DJ/MC at their wedding. It's basic; remember, the easier you make it, the more likely they will book. My advice is using it as a base to create your own document specific to your business. Then have it checked by a qualified solicitor.

Living guest book

These are similar to the forms I ask guests to fill in to create a 'Living guest book' at a wedding reception. You're welcome to photocopy these pages to use yourself, or use them as a template for creating your own version.

Wedding planning forms

This is a suggested form that you can use when meeting with the bride and groom to plan their reception. The idea is to get as much information as possible; this will help you to advise the couple when it comes to planning and staging the reception.

Evaluation Form

This is an unbranded version of a similar form I send out to clients; you're welcome to use it as a reference when putting your own together.

Reception timeline

This is an example for you to use as a guide; when you type yours up make it as easy to read as possible. I will email a copy of this to photographers and videographers ahead of time. Another suggestion is to put one or two copies on the head table, maybe for the best man and maid of honour for a reference, but don't give it to the bride and groom.

Your Company (ENTERTAINMENT) LIMITED

Service Agreement

THE PARTIES: The agreement is for entertainment services for the event described below, between the undersigned purchaser of entertainment (Client) and John Beck (Company).

SERVICES: John Beck confirms he will personally be the Wedding Entertainer MC/DJ. Provide a commercial sound system, music library and labour for the event, in addition to any other specified items.

CLIENT DETAILS

BRIDE AND GROOM'S NAME:_____

CLIENT
ADDRESS_____

_____

Bride-
Email:_____
Groom-
Email_____

PHONE:-BRIDE _____   GROOM_____

EVENT-DATE: _____

FACILITY NAME: _____

ROOM-NAME:_____PHONE: _____

FACILITY
ADDRESS:_____

CONTACT NAME: _____

APPROX.#OF GUESTS:_____MAJORITY AGE RANGE: _____

MUSIC START TIME: _____ END TIME: _____

Total Fee:_____Initial Payment _____Balance Due: _____

$500 initial payment is due and payable upon booking. Balance is due ten (10) days before the Event Date. Payment can be made by cash, cheque, money order or direct deposit using your name as a reference to BSB xxxxxx ACCT. xxxxxxx Cheque(s) should be made payable to: John Beck

This agreement is with_____ Client, and John Beck.

By signing this agreement, it is acknowledged that the Client exercises his/her authority to do so and hereby assume liability for the amount and term stated herein.

MONEY BACK GUARANTEE: If after the event you don't believe you got your money's worth out of my service, I will refund whatever you think is appropriate.

SUBSTITUTES: If, on account of illness of John Beck or any other cause beyond control, a substitute will be provided on the same specified terms and conditions as are stated herein. If John Beck fails to appear at an event without organising a substitute the buyer will receive a total refund plus an extra $100.

REFUND/CANCEL: If client cancels, it must be in writing. If cancellation occurs, the initial payment $500 is non-refundable. But is transferable and applicable to another date within one (1) year of booking.

DAMAGES: Client assumes liability and cost if equipment used by John Beck is damaged by buyer and/or guests. John Beck reserves the right to deny anyone access to property owned by our company.

INSUFFICIENT FUNDS: If client's cheque does not clear for any reason, then client agrees to pay a $30.00 service charge.

OVERTIME: Overtime is calculated in one (1) hour increments and any portion thereof at $150 per hour per performer.

This agreement shall be null and void unless received by John Beck within fourteen (14) days of the agreement date.

CLIENT   SIGNATURE: _____   DATE:
_____

John Beck SIGNATURE: _____
DATE: _____

Please return your signed and dated booking agreement to John Beck PO Box xx Park xxxx , using the enclosed self-addressed stamped envelope.

Once your booking agreement is received, you will receive an email confirmation from me within 48 hours.

ANY ADDITIONAL DETAILS_____

Advice and Suggestions
For The Bride and Groom on Their Wedding Day

"To have a long and happy marriage, I would….

_____

_____ "

Name: _____Relationship to Bride/Groom _____

"The one thing never to say is …

_____

_____ "

Name: _____

Relationship to Bride/Groom _____

"The one thing I'd like to tell the opposite sex is …

_____

_____ "

Name: _____

Relationship to Bride/Groom_____

"The one thing never to do is …

_____

_____ "

Name: _____

Relationship to Bride/Groom _____

Reception Worksheet

Note: After you return this paperwork, I will follow up with you to discuss, and provide feedback regarding your choices. This will help ensure the results you envision.

Date of event   Number of Guests
Ceremony Ending Time   Reception Arrival Time
Reception Start Time   Reception End Time
Name of Room

Please instruct the venue that the DJ will NOT need a table for equipment.
  Done   Not Done

Please provide a floor plan with the return of this document.
  Done   Not done

I'll call seven to ten days before your reception to go over pronunciation of all names and provide feedback to the choices you've made. It's my job to help you in every way possible. Of course I'll always do as you ask, and honour your wishes that fit within the agreement of our contract.

l understand   Don't understand

While respect is given to proper volume, please try to avoid seating sound-sensitive or older people near the DJ speakers. We also want to be sure that people in the back of the room can hear if turned down low.

I understand-   I don't understand

Videographer's first name
Photographer's first name

Playing Music
Of course, the special songs you selected will be played. Following are your options on how all remaining music is to be played.

1) Yes No You're the professional. I prefer to trust your judgment and experience, to choose (program) all music. Fit our songs in when it works best.
2) Yes No Please take song requests from the crowd. I understand this style of playing music does not necessarily ensure satisfaction of the majority of our guests, and may not produce a 'good flow'.

3)Yes no   Please play our song requests before any request you get from the crowd.
4)Yes no   Play any song requests received before our personal requests. Just play ours if there is time.

Standard Order of Events

The following section pertains to all people introduced with music. This is done at the conclusion of cocktail hour and just before dinner.

Grand Entrance Music Song

*In order to be heard clearly and understood well, please be sure to choose a song without lyrics (instrumental). Singing interferes with the MC announcing (it's like two people talking at the same time). I have excellent song recommendations if needed. Refer to the enclosed song list and see the category 'Grand Entrance' on the last page. Highlighted songs in red are highly recommended.

Grand Entrance Introductions

Please provide names of all bridal party members you wish to have announced, as outlined below.

1st set of grandparents of the groom- (If divorced) enter: separately together

2nd set of grandparents of the groom- (If divorced) enter: separately together

1st set of grandparents of the bride- (If divorced) enter: separately together

2nd set of grandparents of the bride- (If divorced) enter: separately together

Parents of the groom- (If divorced) enter: separately together

Parents of the bride- (If divorced) enter: separately together

Flower girl(s)   Ring bearer(s)

Jr. Bridesmaid: Escorted by: (optional, not necessary)

Bridesmaids: Groomsman: Entrance Song:
(Please list in the same order you wish them to be announced)

Maid (single) Matron of Honour (married):

Best Man:

Bride and Groom Entrance song:

The form of your names you wish to use for the grand entrance introduction:
Mr. and Mrs. (groom's name).   and bride's name   (last name)

The form of your name you wish to be addressed by throughout the evening, excluding introductions. (Your nickname or the name people often use to address you):
Groom's first name)

Bride's first name)

Yes- no Dinner Prayer (if yes, by whom)

Yes- no Toast by FOB? First name (or nickname)

Yes- no Maid/Matron of honour or Best man to speak? First name (or nickname)

Yes no List anybody else to be speaking:

Yes no Will groom and/or bride add a few words after toast?

Yes- no lf available, do you approve of the DJ and Emcee eating if there are extra settings? (Many times, extra settings you've paid for are available because some guests you've invited are 'no shows'. You may want to consider the same for the photographer and videographer as well.)
Yes- no Disposable cameras for guests? (Instruction announcement will be made)

Cake Cutting song:

Before dinner entre'   after dinner entre' (recommended)

*NOTE: Following grand entrance some venues try to insist on doing the cake cutting immediately after the grand entrance in order to 'get it out of the way'. Please DO NOT agree with the venue, should they try to insist. You are the client. Your cake slices will 'dry out' before being served because the venue cut them up too soon and they're sitting around too long on plates during the dinner period.

Yes- no Sweet Table: before dancing   during dancing period

I recommend that the sweet table is set up and announced at the conclusion of dinner and before dancing begin. If the sweet table is opened later people will leave the dance floor to enjoy the sweet table. Please be aware that this interruption of dancing could last for up to 30 minutes.

yes _no Father/Daughter Dance: Butterfly Kisses _ Daddy's Little Girl_
Other:

Bride and Groom First Dance: Title   artist

Yes _No Bridal Party Dance:
If you were debating between two songs for the first dance (bride and groom), this would be a great time to do the alternate choice
Name of song   artist name

I understand _Don't understand
If you have a special request during the dancing period, please take time to approach the DJ personally when you're able, rather than sending a messenger (to ensure that it's truly your request). Of course we'll honour your request, while still being careful not to interrupt the programming flow. It is always our intention to honour your wishes as quickly as possible in a professional manner.

Interactive Activity Options
Of course, you and your fiancé are the hosts of this event. Interactivity is primarily intended to provide fun and involvement for your guests. Interactivity also serves as 'ice-breakers' to help loosen up a smaller audience and get the energy up.
For events fewer than 100 guests the more interactivity, the better. For events over 150 it becomes less necessary but still very fun.

Yes- no Nutbush
Yes- no Conga Line: Hot, Hot, Hot   Locomotion
yes- no Bouquet Toss   Song:

Yes- no Shimmy: Leave blank, I'll explain when I call you.

Yes- no Garter Removal   Song

Yes -no 2nd Garter Routine:
Girl who caught the bouquet toss sits in the chair the bride was using during the garter removal. Guy who caught the garter toss must place the garter on the leg of the bouquet toss winner. Very fun!

Yes- no   Mother/ Son Dance: Song

Yes- no Any engagement announcements?
1st couple's name
Wedding date
2nd couple's name
Wedding date

Yes- no Will you be changing clothes during the reception, leaving the reception room for any planned period of time exceeding ten minutes, or leaving the reception early?

Yes- no Chicken Dance
Yes- no Hokey Pokey
Yes- no Any Ethnic Music: e.g. Greek, Italian, Jewish, Latin
Yes- no Time Warp
Yes- no Macarena

Yes- no any birthday announcements?
Yes- no Play Happy Birthday?
Age _   Name   Date
Age_   Name.   Date

Yes- no Generation Dance
Invite all married couples only to slow dance. During the song, couples are intermittently excused from the dance floor based on the number of years they've been married. We ultimately find out who has been married longest. The husband and wife are then asked a question regarding the success of their lengthy marriage. This often produces humorous answers.

161

Yes- no any anniversary announcements?
Husband/wife name
Number of years married

Yes- no Stroll (also known as a Soul Train) Women line up on one side of dance floor, men on the other. Person(s) at front of the line, dance down the centre and get back in line.

Billy Jean
Now that we found love

yes- no The Shoe Game
This game is to show how much the new Mr./Mrs. really knows about each other ... I will ask you a question and you raise the shoe that you think best fits the answer to the question ... all right here's a practice question ..."Right now, who has the most cash on them?"

Yes- no Bus stop
Yes- no Magic Circle Dance
Circle is formed with a dancer in middle. That person chooses his/her replacement (repeat).
Ice Ice Baby
Stayin' Alive

Other group participation dance suggestions
yes- no YMCA
yes- no Shout
yes- no The Twist
yes- no Grease mega mix
yes- no Hula Hoop contest
yes- no Limbo contest

yes- no The Mixer (a social dance)
Two circles, one of men one of women. Women move in a clockwise direction men anticlockwise when music stops you must dance with the person opposite you.

Anything else I need to know?

EVALUATION FORM

We are grateful for your patronage, and would ask your assistance by filling out this evaluation form so that we can continue to maintain our high standards and serve you better.

Function_____ Date of Function _____

1. On your initial phone call (Entertainment) Limited how were you treated?   (please tick)
Friendly _____ Enthusiastically _____ Courteously _____ Rudely _____
Listened to your needs_____ Did not listen _____ Professionally _____
Unprofessionally_____

2. Were your phone calls returned?   Yes _____   No _____

3. Was your consultation (if applicable)
Helpful _____ Enlightening _____ Overbearing _____Unprofessional _____ Listened to your needs _____ Exactly what you wanted_____

4. At the function, how was the Presenter's appearance?
Appropriately dressed _____ Inappropriately dressed _____ Neat and clean _____ Sloppy or untidy_____

5.Describe the Presenter's selection of music for your function:
Exactly what we expected _____ Played a wide variety _____Took requests _____ Did not take requests_____   Could   not   get   people dancing_____

6.How would you describe the Presenter's co-ordination of your function?
Exceeded our expectations _____ Very organised _____ Very unorganised _____ Took charge _____ We had no worries _____ Lost control _____

7.After the performance, what were your feelings about the success of the function?
Extremely   satisfied_____Satisfied   _____Dissatisfied___Extremely dissatisfied_____

8.Did you feel you received value and service for the money you spent?
Yes _____ No _____
If no, why?

_____
_____

9.How would you rate the entertainment value you received for your money?
I would pay slightly less _____   I would pay slightly more _____   I would pay a lot more _____ I would pay the same _____   Worth   every cent _____

10. What amount of importance did the Presenter play in making your function a total success?
10% _____   15% _____   20% _____   25% _____   30% _____   40% _____   50% _____   More _____

11.What would you say was the difference in choosing (Entertainment) Limited over other DJ companies?
_____
_____

12. In your opinion, is there anything we can improve?
_____
_____

13. FAVOURITE MOMENT what did you like most about our service?
_____
_____

14. If you had the opportunity to tell someone what to look for in a DJ service   what   would   that   be?
_____
_____

15.Are you comfortable referring us to family and friends?

Yes _____   No _____

16. May we use your name as a reference?

Yes _____   No _____

Name _____

Phone No _____

Address_____

Reception Timeline
Kaite & Michael Saunders
Saturday 7th June 2014

6:30   canapés pre-dinner drinks

7:00   guests seated
7:05   John welcomes guests

7:10   Bridal party announced
            1. Caitlin & Adam   sexy and I know it
            2. Allie (MOH) & Toby (BM)   Blurred Lines
            3. Mr & Mrs. Michael and Kaite Saunders   Bang Bang

7:19   Short welcome and thank you by Michael Saunders
7:20   Cake Cutting   Grow old with you-Adam Sandler

7:30   entrée served

8:00   Speeches   1. Greg Nicholls (FOB)
                         2. Rex Saunders (FOG)
                         3. Michael Saunders

8:30   Main course served

9:15   First dance   Home-Edward Sharpe & The magnetic zeros
            Bridal Party dance   all on me –John Legend

9:30   Dessert served

9:45   Father/daughter dance   spending my time-Roxette
              Mother/son dance   devil gate drive-Suzi quarto

10:30   Cake and coffee served

11:35   Bouquet throw   girls just wanna have fun
            No garter
11:40   newlywed quiz

11:50   last dance   your arms around me-Jens Lekman
11:55   Michael & Kaite depart

Midnight   function   concludes

34256415R00095

Made in the USA
Lexington, KY
30 July 2014